PENGUIN BOOKS

THE BONE LADY

Mary H. Manhein is director of the Forensic Anthropology and Computer Enhancement Services Laboratory and instructor of anthropology at Louisiana State University. A fellow in the physical anthropology section of the American Academy of Forensic Sciences, she is also deputy coroner of East Baton Rouge Parish.

THE
BONE
LADY

LIFE AS A
FORENSIC
ANTHROPOLOGIST

MARY H. MANHEIN

PENGUIN BOOKS

PENGUIN BOOKS
Published by the Penguin Group
Penguin Group (USA) Inc., 375 Hudson Street, New York, New York 10014, U.S.A.
Penguin Group (Canada), 90 Eglinton Avenue East, Suite 700, Toronto,
    Ontario, Canada M4P 2Y3 (a division of Pearson Penguin Canada Inc.)
Penguin Books Ltd, 80 Strand, London WC2R 0RL, England
Penguin Ireland, 25 St Stephen's Green, Dublin 2, Ireland (a division of Penguin Books Ltd)
Penguin Group (Australia), 250 Camberwell Road, Camberwell,
    Victoria 3124, Australia (a division of Pearson Australia Group Pty Ltd)
Penguin Books India Pvt Ltd, 11 Community Centre, Panchsheel Park, New Delhi – 110 017, India
Penguin Group (NZ), cnr Airborne and Rosedale Roads,
    Albany, Auckland 1310, New Zealand (a division of Pearson New Zealand Ltd)
Penguin Books (South Africa) (Pty) Ltd, 24 Sturdee Avenue,
    Rosebank, Johannesburg 2196, South Africa

Penguin Books Ltd, Registered Offices: 80 Strand, London WC2R 0RL, England

First published in the United States of America by
Louisiana State University Press, 1999
Published in Penguin Books 2000

20 19 18 17 16 15 14 13

THE LIBRARY OF CONGRESS HAS CATALOGED
THE HARDCOVER EDITION AS FOLLOWS:
Manhein, Mary H., 1943–
The bone lady: life as a forensic anthropologist / Mary H. Manhein.
p. cm.
ISBN 0-8071-2404-4 (hc.)
ISBN 0 14 02.9192 X (pbk.)
1. Manhein, Mary H. 1943– .   2. Women forensic anthropologists—Southern States—
Biography.   3. Forensic anthropology—Southern States.   4. Physical anthropology—
Southern States.   5. Human remains (Archaeology)—Southern States.   6. Southern
States—Antiquities.   I. Title.
GN50.6.M35M35   1999
301'.092—dc21   99-17244

Printed in the United States of America
Set in Adobe Garamond
Designed by Amanda McDonald Scallan

To my mother, Madie Withers Huffman, 1918–1984,
for all you were and all you might have been

CONTENTS

ILLUSTRATIONS

ACKNOWLEDGMENTS

For almost two decades I have worked with hundreds of law enforcement agents, locally, nationally, and internationally. Though too numerous to name, they often played vital, even heroic roles in the stories recollected in the following pages. So many times they made the suggestion, "If you ever write a book, Mary, write one that we would like to read." I hope I have succeeded.

In addition, many who influenced this book's creation were participants in the workshops and seminars I conducted throughout the United States. I am grateful for their positive comments.

More specifically, I wish to acknowledge three whose contributions here may be readily identified: Mary Lee Eggart, a remarkable scientific artist, and Kerry Lyle, a gifted photographer, provided, respectively, the drawings and some of the photographs for the text. And the wonderful Assistant Director of Louisiana State University Press, Maureen Hewitt, has my special thanks for seeing immediately what I was trying to accomplish in writing this book.

On a personal level, I want to acknowledge several friends who inspired me: Eileen Barrow, Beth Bassett, Maria Cashion-Lugo, Sandy Calloway, Sheila Faulkenberry, Saundra Henderson, Ann Ingram, Ginny Listi, Kathleen Marshall, Lamar Meek, Ann Marie Mires, Hampton Peele, T. O. Perry, Paula Cannon Porter, Miles Richardson, George Schiro, Paula Sheperd, Ann Whitmer, Larry Wilson, and Leah Wood.

In particular, I owe a debt of gratitude to my friend David Madden, Director of the United States Civil War Center, who believed in me from the beginning and who has encouraged me greatly throughout the last few years. His editorial comments helped in essential ways to shape this book.

Finally, I thank my family: my husband's parents, Mary Dee and William Manhein, for making me feel so special; my sister, Ella Garren, to whom I owe my life itself; my sons, Andy and Trey, and my daughter-in-law, Kelly, for listening to all the early drafts and laughing at the parts I hoped were humorous; my niece, Missy Dodson, for her belief in my work; and my husband, Bill, for always encouraging me. I am grateful to be surrounded by so much love in my adult life.

THE
BONE
LADY

INTRODUCTION

"The Bone Lady" is the nickname I acquired from law enforcement personnel while working with authorities from most of the sixty-four parishes in Louisiana, several counties in Texas, Arkansas, and Mississippi, and various agencies across the country. In more formal terms, I am a forensic anthropologist and bioarchaeologist, a scientist who works with human bones in a medico-legal context and who sometimes digs them up.

The idea for *The Bone Lady* started years ago when I began to notice and appreciate the widespread interest the general public has in forensic anthropology and bioarchaeology. My purpose in writing this book was to share my passion for anthropology with others while telling the human stories behind my cases, stories that are often fragmented and incomplete. Though a scientist by trade, by birth and "ascribed status," as we anthropologists say, I am also a storyteller.

I come from the hills of southwest Arkansas and northwest Louisiana, where my life revolved around stories. A friend once said to me that he felt the reason that I was successful in later years as a college teacher was that I was able to weave a story into every lesson I taught.

The desire to share stories goes back to my childhood when my family would spend hours around the fireplace, just inside the ring of light, listening to the storytellers. My favorite tales were those told by my mother and my Aunt Penny. Memories of those stories come to me at the oddest of times. I find them comforting.

Stories, myths, legends, memories of the past—all are part of what makes us who we are. They give us a sense of place. "Place" for me is in those hills. From there I recall the stories of my youth and, consciously and unconsciously, incorporate them into who and what I am. My past in the hills is woven into this book, sometimes in fond remembrance, and other times, in joy, that it is just that, the past.

I was born in those hills on the blustery winter solstice of 1943—"on the cusp," as astrologers say—and, as with all but two of Mama's ten children, at home. My father's one lung and skill at pumping sand from the Red River kept him stateside during World War II and brought me into this world. I was a "war baby," not a "baby boomer," those babies born after the war was over when soldiers returned home. I have no real memories of "the last good war," but I do remember clearly my brief years in my hometown.

For the first seven years of my life, we lived in three rooms of the old "company hotel" on the outskirts of Lewisville, Arkansas, at the railroad switchyard. We shared the first floor with Mama's sister, Pearl, and her family. The hotel's abandoned second floor, where we often played, contained nooks and crannies filled with dusty, broken furniture. When a train rumbled through the switchyard, all the windows shook with an eerie, death-rattle sound. Following the war for a brief period of time a few sick men in beds lived on the second floor of the hotel. I would cling to Mama's skirts as she walked back and forth talking to them and feeding them. I don't know who they were.

Author with brother Buddy *(left)* and cousin Danny *(right)* at railroad switchyard

The trains brought strange men to our door. They were always hungry. Mama said their numbers increased after the war. She never let them in the house but she never turned one away. She made every one a plate of food from whatever she had, and he sat on the side steps to eat his meal. I peeked at these men from a safe distance as they licked their fingers and sometimes even their plates. Occasionally, I also watched one hop another train when it slowed or stopped at the switchyard, waving a faint good-bye.

My father's three brothers and three of Mama's brothers went to the war. They all came back, a couple of them coming to visit us. I remember racing down the dirt road with my brother and sister to meet them, looking so serious in the dark, scratchy uniforms they wore long after the war was over.

I could read before I started first grade in the post–World War II rural South; Mama's Bible was my primer. In the fall of 1949 she convinced the school board that regardless how small her ragamuffin daughter was, she would not hold her out for another year on the off-chance that she might grow more. Good thing—it would be years before my feet could reach the floor at my desk, and from class to class I carried the little green footrest that the school janitor made for me so my dangling legs and feet would not go to sleep.

I was hungry to learn and took in everything my teachers said. However, our transient life-style over the years sometimes made it difficult to keep up with others in my grade. The greatest continuity in my teenage years came with our three-year stay on the outskirts of the small town of Ida in northwest Louisiana, population 367.

Our family was packed into a three-room shotgun house with no plumbing. Such a house is just one room wide. With all the doors open, a shotgun blast could go through the front door and out the back without damage to the structure. Though, personally, I never tested that theory, to stay in one place was a godsend. I had attended three schools in as many months that year. From coastal Morgan City to rural Bayou Black and back to the hills of north Louisiana, we transported our meager belongings.

It was in Ida that I was introduced to the dynasty of perhaps the most famous Louisianian of all, Governor Huey Long. The introduction came through "Uncle Earl," Huey's baby brother. All our lives

Mama had told stories about Huey Long and his family. To the poor in rural Louisiana, he was a god. Free schoolbooks, decent roads, and voting rights were just a few of his reported legacies that Mama held dear. My image of Huey Long and his sibling was herculean. I had no idea that some thirty-five years later I would search for graves and excavate burials on the very grounds of the great Capitol complex Huey Long had built in Baton Rouge and a year after that mull over the bones of his alleged assassin, Dr. Carl Austin Weiss.

It was around 1959 when Earl Kemp Long's "stumping" brought him to Ida late one afternoon. Stumping was an informal style of campaigning that had gained popularity in the days of Huey Long. Adapting the soapbox strategy, Huey and other politicians would stand on tree stumps among rural workers in order to be seen and heard.

When I hopped from the school bus that day, Mama was waiting beside the road. "Mr. Earl's down at Carroway's grocery," she said, "talking about the upcoming election." I knew he was campaigning for some office, and I took off, racing the mile and a half into town. Mama wouldn't go. Gathered on the steps at Carroway's was a small group of people and a short, dumpy man whom I felt could not possibly be a Long. I anxiously scanned the crowd for the brother of Mama's hero.

"That's not Mr. Earl," I said to someone. "Where is he?"

"I think he's down at the cafe," came the reply.

I ran across the street and entered the darkened room, the screen door slapping softly against my sweat-covered shirt as I adjusted my eyes to the shadows. The soft whine of the ceiling fan was the only sound in the almost empty space. At a small corner table sat a wizened little man in khaki pants and a white shirt with his sleeves rolled up. He was leaning into the table and sipping on a Coca-Cola through a straw.

"Are you Mr. Earl?" I said, hoping he could not detect the disappointment in my voice.

"Yes I am, little lady."

"Could I have your autograph?" I whispered, grabbing one of the cheap, white paper napkins from a nearby canister.

"Of course," he said.

I do not remember what Earl Long wrote that day—something brief. I slipped from the room as quickly and quietly as I had entered, squinting at the edge of the evening sun just above the tree line. I walked slowly down the street. Turning the corner, I stopped on the railroad overpass bridge as a train came rumbling from the north. I looked at the train and began to tear the napkin, first in half, then into quarters, and then into eighths as it slipped from my fingers and into the wind. I told Mama Mr. Earl was shorter than I thought he would be.

Almost twenty years would pass before I entered college and headed toward my professional collision with the Longs. Marriage, two sons, and a job transfer for my husband down to Baton Rouge came in-between. In 1976, when the younger of my sons entered kindergarten, I announced to everyone that I was "matriculating," using a word that I would never use again, plucked for the moment from the pages of the *Louisiana State University General Catalog*.

One of my favorite subjects in high school had been English. I chose that as a college major. College immediately became a source of accomplishment and a constant juggling act to schedule classes around my children's school hours. Super mom made cupcakes for grade-school programs, cheered on the kids' ball teams, stayed up half the night encouraging brain synapses to fire, and waited impatiently in rainy-day carpool lines while reading Shakespeare and Salinger.

A slight setback came in my junior year with a broken foot I sustained in a badminton game during a course fulfilling one of my curriculum's physical activities requirements. I was playing for the championship in the class competition when I went up to ace my last shot and win the match. The not-so-happy twenty-year-old male on the other side of the net was as surprised as I that I had made it that far in the first place when my foot caught in the artificial surface of the field house and sent me sprawling. I had to forfeit the match. I like to think I might have won that day. What I remember most about my first and only broken bone was scooting backward up the stairs to the second floor in Allen Hall for a poetry class with a backpack on my back, my crutches banging the wall as I went. A gallant young man offered to carry me, but, unfortunately, I refused my one opportunity to play Scarlett in jeans.

I took a variety of courses the university had to offer. From philosophy to geology, I vigorously debated everything. Questions in medical ethics, such as who gets the first available kidney (the rich or the poor?), intrigued me as much as questions in geology (is the earth 6,000 or 4.5 billion years old?). I settled on "first come, first serve" on the kidney and accepted that "old as dirt" could be quite old indeed.

At thirty-seven, as a senior with plans to graduate in the spring of 1981, I had the luxury of taking a few last-minute electives during my final two semesters. I was still looking for something—I didn't know what—even as I looked forward to graduation. I had ignored anthropology in general, not knowing much about it. My peers, a group of mature females, who were few and far between on campus at that time, had not taken any anthropology courses. When I asked them what they had heard about anthropology, they labeled it "interesting but difficult." That did it; I signed up immediately for a senior-level course in Old World archaeology. After just three weeks, I was hooked. By the end of the semester, after only one course, all I could think was, "Where have you been all my life, anthropology?"

I had found a field that focused on the cultural and physical attributes of man and woman, one that was filled with puzzles and mysteries. The next semester I applied to enter the master's program in anthropology in the Department of Geography and Anthropology at Louisiana State University (LSU).

Prior to entering graduate school in the fall of 1981, I participated in my first summer archaeology field school. It was an eye-opener. Armed with shiny new Red Wing work boots and my very own Marshalltown trowel into whose blade had been blasted my initials, I headed for the hills of Louisiana to "dig." An abbreviated, two-week summer field school had been organized in conjunction with the regular university archaeological field school at a prehistoric, Native American site called Poverty Point in Epps. With my young sons ensconced at their grandmother's house for a couple of weeks, I began my life as an anthropologist. Up before dawn, in the field by daylight, digging in Louisiana clay all day; centimeter by centimeter in neat little squares, in deep, big holes, we were trying to find our way to the past. I thought, with some irony, "Didn't I leave these dirt hills behind years ago?"

I made lasting friends that summer. Occasionally, we still share a dirt hole together, a cold beer, and a few memories of the time in 1981 when, coincidentally, Harrison Ford melted our hearts in *Raiders of the Lost Ark* and turned many a head toward archaeology.

Halfway into my first year of graduate school, I reviewed the four subdisciplines of anthropology: archaeology, cultural anthropology, linguistic anthropology, and physical anthropology. I made the decision to combine the two subdisciplines of archaeology and physical anthropology into what some people refer to today as the fifth subdiscipline: applied anthropology, where anthropologists work outside of academia—in my case, forensic anthropology.

One of the major credentials that establishes a "real" forensic anthropologist, acknowledged professionally in the field, is membership in the American Academy of Forensic Sciences. By 1998 the Academy had more than 4,500 members from various disciplines, including biology and pathology, criminalistics, psychology, and toxicology. Approximately 100 of us worldwide are full, voting members of the Academy under a section designated "Physical Anthropology." Our section, one of the smallest in the Academy, was established in the 1970s. New, regular members to this group enter through a process of invitation and peer review and have attained at least a master's degree in anthropology (with a concentration in physical anthropology), as well as establishing a history of forensic case loads and making other contributions to the field. The highest level of distinction among the regular members to the Academy is that of "fellow." As of late 1998, around thirty-five of us worldwide hold that honor in the physical anthropology section.

Board certification in forensic anthropology is also available to physical anthropologists with doctorates. Academy membership and board certification are voluntary. Though desirable, these credentials are not essential for a physical anthropologist to become a practicing forensic anthropologist. When law enforcement seeks the aid of a forensic anthropologist, ethics and experience in the field are the requisite qualifications.

Now as an instructor in anthropology, I advise undergraduate and graduate students from all over the United States. When these prospective students contact me for information about this unique discipline, I explain how few of us there are, how more of us who can assist law enforcement are needed in the country, and how Academy membership—even at the student level—can be beneficial to their careers. I also note the work's drawbacks. I tell them, "If you don't mind low pay, night and weekend work, treacherous recovery sites, snakes, mosquitoes, and poison ivy, then a career in forensic anthropology and bioarchaeology could give you amazing job satisfaction." They know by the sound of my voice what it has given me.

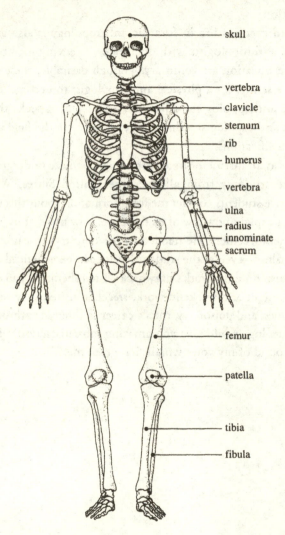

skull

vertebra

clavicle

sternum

rib

humerus

vertebra

ulna

radius

innominate

sacrum

femur

patella

tibia

fibula

Human skeleton

BEHIND THE LEVEE

ON the first day of the search, I failed to find the body. The informant said we would find the man in a black plastic bag. Willie Dulac* thought he knew where he had dug the hole for the man in the bag, but he wasn't absolutely sure and it had been five years. He leaned against a small willow tree and watched us, his thin, nervous hands tightly gripping a rotting branch. His cheek twitched just a little as the backhoe dipped its long arm into the soft mud and came up empty, again.

Lt. Jennie May of the Louisiana State Police had called me that morning back in 1990 at my laboratory at Louisiana State University in Baton Rouge (LSU) and asked for my help in the case. As the only forensic anthropologist within hundreds of miles at the time, I routinely got such calls. This one would prove to be a little different.

*Here and throughout the text, names of all victims and criminals have been changed.

Willie Dulac trapped snakes and lizards for a living, and he lived from day to day. Willie had more problems, however, than meeting his weekly quota of reptiles. He was scared. He was scared because he shared a secret known only to one other person, his nephew Jacob. Willie had helped Jacob to bury Duncan Morgan, sealed in a black plastic bag, on the banks of the mighty Mississippi River almost five years earlier. Willie didn't kill him; he just buried him. Jacob had been in prison for another crime for most of the years since the burial had taken place, but he was getting out soon. Willie knew that Jacob, nephew or no, would not risk going back to prison for the life of one snake charmer. Willie informed.

The Louisiana State Police had been wanting to get Jacob for years. He was thought to have participated in a variety of heinous crimes, and they wanted to put him away for a long, long time. Jacob knew they wanted him, and in recent years, his Christmas cards to some of the law enforcement agents with the greeting "see you when I get out" brought a little discomfort to their lives, to say the least.

However, the recovery team encountered a problem. It was late winter, and the banks of the river were slippery, cold, muddy, and misleading. Buried bodies can be a challenge to the most experienced forensic anthropologist. If buried deeply enough, there are only two ways a deliberate burial will be found: by accident or by the aid of an informant, preferably one with a good memory.

The State Police knew they had another problem: Willie could flee. If he did, they might never find the body or prosecute the man whom they believed blew off Duncan Morgan's head while he watched television from his brown vinyl recliner in the rickety trailer he called home. Parked just north of Houston in a two-row trailer camp, the abandoned trailer with bullet-riddled walls was a stark reminder that the police had no body to identify or to bury. All they had was Willie Dulac and his incredible story . . . and the possibility that he might flee at any moment.

In such burial cases, backhoes can be very helpful because they can move large amounts of dirt quickly. They enable a recovery team to cover broad areas without becoming exhausted from sometimes futile hand shoveling. A skilled backhoe operator can skim topsoil a few centimeters at a time, often revealing the near-surface outline of an elusive burial, whether it's archaeological or forensic in nature. However, as beneficial as they are, backhoes cannot work miracles, especially in areas where watery holes mislead at every turn and even confound the one who originally dug the clandestine grave.

So there I was. Amid fire ants, rising water, and prison trusty labor, we built sandbag levees, and we looked and looked for the man in the plastic bag, but we couldn't find him. We finally stopped digging that day behind the levee near the river's edge, deciding to wait until the banks dried up a little, hoping that Willie would not flee.

Three weeks later, on a bright, sunny spring day, the banks became more manageable. As our backhoe moved across the muddy river bank, its tracks sinking deeply into the watery soil, it accidentally clipped the edge of a black plastic bag.

I hurried to the scene and borrowed a knife to slit open the bag, which obviously held something big and heavy. Not knowing the condition of what lay inside, I decided to have a "look-see" to determine whether the remains should be shipped to the morgue for autopsy or transported directly to my laboratory for osteological analysis. Five years in the ground created intriguing possibilities for a body's preservation. Slowly I began to cut, pausing momentarily to step back and take one last, long breath of fresh air before lifting the edge of the bag.

The remains were partially intact; pink soft tissue could be seen in the lower limb region. Adipocere, a brownish-white, soaplike material, was everywhere. It often forms in a moist environment from the postmortem hydrolysis of body fat and the mummification of muscle and other tissues. The strong odor of decay spread quickly across the scene; grown men turned and walked away.

I knew that important evidence might be lost if that much tissue were preserved and no autopsy effort were made. The borrowed knife was refused by its lender, and, as is often the case, a new tool was added to our field kit of hodgepodge donations. "Take it to the pathologist," I said. Pausing, I added, "And send him my sympathy." I stripped the plastic gloves from my hands, the smell of death lingering on my fingertips.

The pathologist on call that day will not soon forget this case. Though much of the remains were intact, autopsy provided only peripheral information. It was obvious to even a layman that the head was in a hundred pieces. No positive identification using dental records likely would be forthcoming: extensive antemortem tooth loss and bone deterioration I had seen in the jaw probably indicated that the victim had no dental records on file anywhere. The body was rebagged a day later and transported to me, its seductive odor forever permeating the vehicle in which it rode.

When a forensic case comes to my lab at LSU—that is, the Forensic Anthropology and Computer Enhancement Services (FACES) Laboratory where I serve as director—we first describe its condition "on arrival" before photographing and X-raying it. After that, we remove any putrefactive soft tissue that is still attached in order to get to the bone. A careful preliminary assessment of case number 90-3—our third case received in 1990—revealed startling evidence: though disarticulated, or disassociated from the body, two fingers were still intact. The ridges on the skin were visible with the naked eye. "What if the State Police Crime Lab could lift these prints?" I said, almost to myself, more than a little excited at the possibility that the victim might have prints somewhere to match. It was our lucky day. Forensic scientists at the Crime Laboratory captured the prints and matched them to old prints belonging to the victim. He was exactly who Willie said he would be; Duncan Morgan had been found. An arrest and charge could be made.

At this point, the real work for me had just begun. To clean the skeleton, describe multiple episodes of trauma, photograph the remains, and prepare a formal report for law enforcement can take hundreds of hours. The Morgan case was no exception. first, I removed the decaying tissue with sharp scalpel blades and heated water loaded with detergents. Then I laid out the bones in neat rows on metal trays beneath the fume hood to dry them before analysis. Painstakingly, I glued the jagged pieces of the cranium, or skull, back together. Though technically, the "skull" actually refers to the cranium and the mandible, or lower jaw, most people refer to just the cranium as the skull. These two terms have become interchangeable in popular literature.

The ease with which the pieces of the skull fit together distinguished the wounds as having resulted from high-velocity impact rather than the low velocity of blunt force. Often, in blunt force trauma, the bones of the skull are warped and do not reconstruct so easily. As each piece of Duncan Morgan's skull fit into place, a pattern emerged. The wound to the right frontal bone, or forehead, displayed small, characteristic, circular edges to the outer surface of the skull, a projectile's signature. On the inner surface, or table, of the skull, the damage was greater, producing what is often referred to as "internal beveling," or shelving. The trauma to the frontal region was an entry wound.

The rest of Morgan's skull had exploded into tens of fragments. The skull is under considerable internal pressure. Research has shown that, on occasion, fractures to the skull produced by high-velocity projectiles may move faster through the bone than the projectile itself. Other research has provided clues for understanding time of occurrence of multiple traumatic events. Much like the cracks in a vehicle's broken windshield, fractures produced by subsequent bullet wounds usually do not cross primary fracture lines produced by the first projectile. Of course, the greater the damage to the bone, the harder it is to determine sequence of events.

Following my work on Morgan's skull, I moved on to his postcranial remains, all of those bones below the skull. The right scapula, or shoulder blade, was ripped like paper, the jagged edges of the bone in-

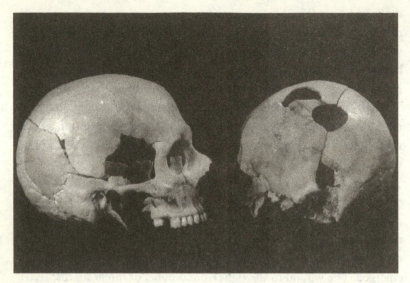

Examples of perimortem trauma: high velocity *(left)* and blunt force *(right)*

clined toward the back of the body in what forensic anthropologists call a hinge fracture. The trauma was ventral to dorsal, or from the front of his body toward the back. Several ribs were cracked and broken. Someone had come at Morgan from his right side, and his skeleton revealed the grim story of his final moments.

Ultimately, the case ended up in court. The murder allegedly had taken place in Texas; the body clearly had been "dumped" in Louisiana; the trial would be held in Houston.

A Harris County assistant district attorney called me one day long before the trial and informed me in a matter-of-fact message that my testimony "would be required." My heart raced with his words, both in excitement and in dread. Every expert witness has a first time in court; I only hoped I would survive mine without permanent scars.

The assistant DA met me at my office a few months later to discuss the case wearing cowboy boots and what surely must have been a ten-gallon hat. The image I had constructed from my phone conversations with the long, tall, handsome, Texas lawyer never wavered; his 6-foot, 5-inch frame boasted a broad, heart-melting smile and an obviously remarkable femur.

Generally in such cases, forensic anthropologists are called to testify for the prosecution, mainly because it is law enforcement who consults us in the first place. Expert witnesses, unlike other witnesses, are allowed to provide "an opinion" with regard to their particular area of expertise. Ethically, we must be neutral and objective in our testimony; sometimes that works in favor of the prosecution and sometimes not. Of course, both sides want to win, but a forensic anthropologist cannot become a willing pawn for either one.

Jim Churchman, a senior forensic scientist and trace evidence expert at the State Police Crime Laboratory, flew to Houston with me for the trial. He would testify on the fingerprints. I would handle the bone.

The heavy, polished doors separated the sparsely populated courtroom from those who waited impatiently on the hard oak benches near its entrance. Witnesses paraded back and forth that day. Some looked scared, others defiant, still others relieved. The air felt heavy with the weight of the past. For hours I watched with curiosity from my station on the bench, wondering what role each had played in the life of the victim or the accused. Expert witnesses are not allowed to hear any testimony until they give theirs and are then dismissed by the judge. Occasionally, we are sequestered, or separated, from other witnesses, sometimes spending hours in small holding rooms, but not that day.

Finally, it was my turn on the stand. The defense attorney "stipulated," or accepted, my credentials. As the prosecution laid out its case against Jacob, I carefully described for the jury the procedure that I follow in my analysis.

I began my testimony in my usual speaking style, rapid-fire delivery paired with a strong southern accent—a strange blend that puz-

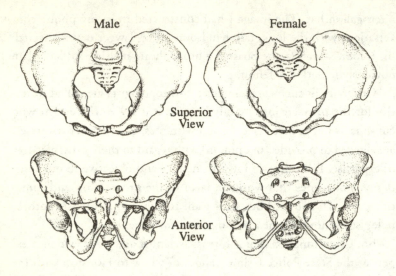

Male   Female

Superior
View

Anterior
View

Male versus female pelves

zles my linguistics colleagues. This brought a silent plea from the court reporter to the judge. Admonishing me, the judge said, "Slow it down a bit, Ms. Manhein. I don't know what you do over in Louisiana, but over here we speak a little more slowly."

"Sorry, Your Honor," I said, my face on fire. "They do in Louisiana, too."

I took a deep breath and began once again. As though teaching my introductory course in physical anthropology at LSU, at a slow, controlled pace I explained in precise language how we establish our skeletal profile. My job on the stand is to lay out my analysis before the jury without a lot of unexplained scientific jargon.

"The shape of the hip bone tells me the remains are those of a male," I noted. Pointing out the features on photographs as I went along, I described how a narrow sciatic notch, a short pubic bone, and a small pelvic inlet, or bowl, all indicated that the hip belonged to a male.

I then moved on to age determination. "The surface of the auricular region of the hip bone, where the hip bone joins the sacrum, is pitted heavily and has uneven borders. This suggests an age over sixty years," I explained. That area had gone through dramatic alterations in appearance with advancing age, changing from a youthful, solid joint surface to a ragged region. "Similar aging changes have occurred to the pubic symphysis, where the hip bones meet in the front of the body," I said with a final gesture.

Then came the main reason I was sitting in the oak-paneled courthouse hundreds of miles from home: to describe the trauma to Mor-

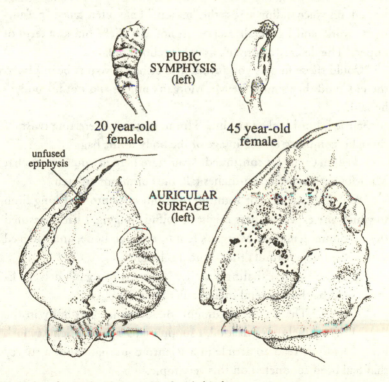

Examples of age-related changes in female hip bones

gan's body. Colored slides of the skull flashed back and forth across a screen, members of the jury wincing at the fractured remains as I advanced the remote control. Black-and-white photographs of broken bones passed through twelve pairs of hands; twenty-four eyes looked deeply into mine as I pointed to my right shoulder blade for a guide and described the hinge fracture to the scapula. Systematically clicking off the last moments of a dying man, I quickly scanned the defense table looking for the "hardened criminal."

The defendant's attorney did not successfully challenge my testimony on the trauma that day, nor could he credibly refute that the fingerprints were the victim's. However, near the close of his crossexamination, his argument took a different tone. "Excuse me, ma'am," he said, his voice sliding across the "ma'am." I am often called "ma'am" in my work, and I generally accept it, not as a cliché but as a term of respect. The defense attorney's use of it echoed hollow.

"Could those fingers you found in that bag have just been placed there? Could they simply be Mr. Morgan's fingers and not his body?" he said.

Startled, I just looked at him. "Hmm, that's an interesting twist," I thought, conjuring up the image of the body in the bag.

"Well, ma'am," he continued, "you state here in your report that Mr. Morgan was 5-feet, 10-inches tall, plus or minus an inch."

"Yes," I answered, not wanting to climb out onto that long limb to which any expert witness might be found clinging. I had measured the maximum length of Morgan's femur, or thigh bone, and plugged that figure into a formula that estimates height.

He began again, exhaling heavily, "Duncan Morgan's driver's license says that he is several inches taller than that."

"That's it? That's your argument for someone else's body in the bag?" I thought, almost out loud. I suppressed a sigh of relief. My luck held. I had just read an article in a scientific journal about a survey that had been conducted on this very topic.

"The results of a recent scientific study reveal that males often *over*report their height on their driver's license; females often *under*-report their weight," I explained. "The fact is, I have not weighed 115 pounds in twenty years, but it sure looks good when I read it on that little card."

The jury laughed out loud.

Willie's nephew, Jacob, was eventually convicted. Later at the trial he was pointed out to me as the tall, thin, meticulously groomed older man in a three-piece business suit whom I took for the senior defense counsel. He is now behind bars—again.

LOST FROM THE *MV MOLLYLEA*

I gently removed the fragile bones from the brown paper bag. The sheriff's deputy shifted his footing to get a little closer to the table as I picked up the skull and stared into its sand-filled cavities.

It was the summer of 1992, and Donnie Gray had been riding his horse on a sandbar along the Mississippi River in Pointe Coupee Parish, just outside the town of New Roads. When Donnie glanced down at the ground in the sparsely wooded area, the deputy recounted, he spotted what looked like a human skull. Upon closer examination, he was certain. The skull and other bones collected by the Pointe Coupee Parish Sheriff's Department made their way to my laboratory at LSU to become case number 92-15, one of a growing list of more than 450 such cases handled by FACES by mid-1998.

"It's a male," I announced, touching each of the features as I scanned the bony sphere. "He has a prominent brow ridge, a sloping forehead, blunt borders on his upper eye sockets (as opposed to sharp upper borders found in females), and large muscle attachment areas."

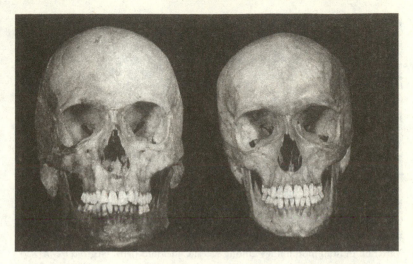

Variation in skull morphology between sexes: male *(left)* and female *(right)*

The shape of the skull also indicated that he was Caucasoid, or white European. His eye orbits were somewhat oval and looked like horizontal teardrops; his nasal opening was narrow and tall; his anterior nasal spine, the small bony projection just below the nose, was quite long.

"He's young—between eighteen and twenty-five—his bones have not quite finished growing," I said, my gaze falling to the youthful looking collarbone. Its medial end (that closest to the midline of the body) exhibited the raised ridges associated with a young adult.

A closer look at the young white male's upper jaw revealed two porcelain crowns on his central incisors, or front teeth. "An easy way to identify him," I thought.

"Look at the color of his bone," I said, speaking to the deputy and to myself, as I continued my preliminary assessment. "It's weathered and has lost its ivory finish and smooth texture." Its grayish color was a sign that it had been exposed on the ground's surface for quite some time, perhaps as long as four or more years.

The sheriff had his osteological profile: young white male with

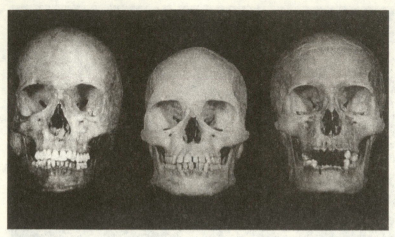

Variation in skull morphology among races: Caucasoid *(left)*, Negroid *(center)*, and Mongoloid (here Asian, *right*)

good dental work who had been dead for at least four years. He could begin the search.

Local and regional missing-persons cases provided the names of several missing youths, some with major dental repair work on their front teeth. Their records, however, did not match our case. Frustrated, the sheriff decided to contact the U.S. Coast Guard, a valuable source of information on missing-persons cases along the waterways. The Coast Guard officials searched their records for persons who had been lost on the river and unaccounted for. Ultimately, Michael Baldwin's name came up in their search. This is Michael's story.

When Michael Baldwin's alarm woke him at 5:30 on the morning of March 14, 1988, he could not know that he would not be cooking breakfast for the rest of the tugboat crew on the *Mollylea* as it slowly headed south on the Mississippi River. Nor did he know that it would be his last day on earth. He may have slipped out of his sleeping quarters, walking up on deck to smoke a cigarette or stopping to check one of the barges the tug was moving slowly downriver. At around 7:00

that same morning, perhaps the rest of the crew began to wonder why they could not detect the familiar aroma of coffee brewing or smell the sweet scent of bacon frying in the pan. A search of the vessel provided no clues. Michael Baldwin had simply disappeared.

By 1992 Baldwin, a twenty-one-year-old white male, had been missing for almost five years, presumably falling overboard from the *Mollylea* that March morning in 1988. He had shipped out of Vicksburg as usual on the *Mollylea* and had been lost, it was believed, somewhere below Natchez, Mississippi.

The Coast Guard officials were able to locate some dental records on Michael because he had previously served in the military. At my request, they forwarded the records to me, but the records were sparse. They included a single radiograph called a Panarex, a type of dental X ray that typically spans the entire upper and lower dental arcades in a wraparound fashion. Unfortunately, the radiograph was faded. We thought we had a positive identification, but we had to be absolutely sure. I noted that case 92-15 had amalgam fillings in the lower jaw teeth, or molars. These often dull, gray fillings are common, but generally, before such fillings are made, smaller X rays, called "bitewings"—which look a lot like blank, postage-sized, plastic rectangles— are taken. These X rays provide a closer look at the tooth to be filled and were exactly what Drs. Robert Barsley and Ronald Carr, odontologists, or forensic dentists, with whom I often consult, needed to confirm a positive identification. I called the Coast Guard and discussed the possibility that other records for Michael existed; they assured me they had everything. I thought of a mother somewhere, waiting, waiting.

"Look," I said, "do you have any objection to my talking to the archives people just one more time? The bitewings are so small; they might have been missed."

"Go ahead," the young officer replied, reciting the telephone number of the military archives in Missouri.

I quickly dialed the number in Missouri and had reeled off a string of questions before the operator could get out, "Hold for archives, please."

The young records clerk with whom I was eventually connected listened patiently as I explained the situation to her.

"Ms. Manhein," she said, "I gave the Coast Guard those records no more than five days ago."

"I know," I replied. "But could you look just one more time? There's a mother in New York who does not know the whereabouts of her son and she's been looking for him for such a long time."

The records clerk promised to look again and call me right back; she did, the excitement building in her voice as she spoke. "I found them, the bitewings, but I can't send them directly to you." They first had to go through the Coast Guard.

I anxiously awaited their arrival in the plain manila envelope with the stilted black lettering. When they reached me, I drove to the LSU Dental School in New Orleans where Doctors Barsley and Carr confirmed what we already knew. Michael Baldwin could go home.

Michael's remains were taken by special courier home to New York. His mother's letter came a short time later. "I said good-bye to Michael last night, and we buried him today beside his grandfather," she wrote. "My heart is broken, but I want to thank you; for the first time in five years, I have peace. Now, when the doorbell rings, I will no longer believe that it could be my son."

SIS

PEOPLE often ask me, "Just what is a forensic anthropologist?" We are physical anthropologists who are trained in the human skeleton, and we use that training in a medico-legal context to assist law enforcement. This assistance sometimes comes when the traditional means used by medical examiners or coroners to autopsy a body after death are no longer applicable. Typically, bones are all that remain to tell the story. However, more often than not these days, we receive many cases that are more than just bone.

As a general rule, forensic anthropologists provide a profile for the police to try to narrow the field in the identification process. We assess age, sex, and race of the person. We also calculate the person's height and look for signs of trauma. finally, we give a statement about time elapsed since death.

Part of our job is what we call the process of elimination. We want

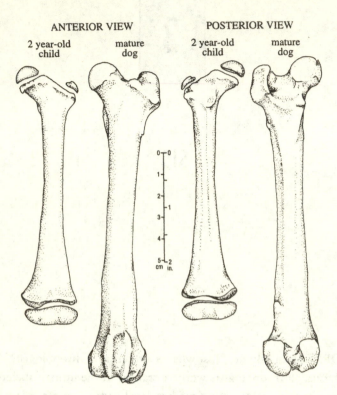

ANTERIOR VIEW   POSTERIOR VIEW

2 year-old   mature   2 year-old   mature
child   dog   child   dog

Animal versus human femora (all bones are from left leg)

to figure out first of all if the material that we are asked to examine is human or animal—easy enough if the bone is complete, not so easy if not.

In formal taxonomic terms, we humans are in the class called Mammalia. The name alludes to the distinction that all mammals have milk-producing mammary glands. Additionally, mammals are warm blooded, have heterodontic, or specialized, teeth, and have similarities in morphology, or skeletal anatomy. The femur of a deer, for instance, when broken or partially burned, can look very similar to the thigh bone of man. Such resemblances in morphology cause identification problems and bring a wide array of skeletal remains to my laboratory.

I received a phone call in the lab one day from a rather excited Chuck Smith, senior coroner's investigator and a deputy coroner for East Baton Rouge Parish. He asked for "the Bone Lady," and the secretary, used to such calls, immediately switched him to my office. He wanted to know if I could meet him in the suburbs to examine something that had been discovered by a man who was digging a drainage trench in his backyard. When the man reached a depth of about three feet, his shovel struck the corner of what appeared to be a wooden box. After he uncovered the box and lifted it from the hole, he became concerned and called the police.

By the time I arrived at the scene, the usual gathering was there: the coroner's investigator, the local police, the sheriff's department, the neighbors, and half the news media in town. Dropping to my knees near the small box, I noted that it was approximately two feet long, one foot wide, and one foot deep. It was well constructed of old cedar and could have remained intact in the backyard's moist environment for hundreds of years.

On top of the box was one cause of the homeowner's concern: the name stamped out in plastic label tape, "Patsy Lou Bates—Sis." Inside the box was darkened soil that had filtered in through the cracks. It had turned to mud due to recent rains. Inside the box also was the main source of the man's concern: a small pile of fragile skeletal remains. They were deep brown because bone is porous and will become similar in color to the soil around it after several years of burial. This is especially true in some parts of south Louisiana where we have a lot of dark clay in our soil, frequently referred to as "gumbo." In contrast, the iron-rich, red clay of central and north Louisiana can stain the bone an orange-red.

I looked closely at the bones for a couple seconds and sighed with relief. I knew beyond doubt that they were not human, though humanlike. I picked up one of the small leg bones, noting that it was about three or four inches long. The ends of the bone were fused and growth had stopped years before. If the bones had been human and that size, the ends, or epiphyses, would have been unattached. Some parts would have been cartilage still and most likely would have completely deteriorated.

"You have a cat or a dog here," I said. "I can be more exact when I get a chance to clean the bones and look at my comparative collection in the lab." The street could return to its routine.

A few days later, I received a phone call from a stranger who had a hard time explaining what she wanted because she was laughing so hard. I finally was able to get to the point of her call. She was the former owner of the house where Sis was found, now living in another state, and had read the writeup about the incident in the local newspaper that someone had sent to her. She said, "You were so right! Those bones were the remains of our family pet, our toy Manchester dog, and she lived to a ripe old age." Her family obviously attached great sentiment to their pets and had given that particular one a human name.

"In addition," she informed me, "if someone moves over a few more feet and continues digging, he is going to discover Bitsy, our other family pet. I just thought you would like to know before they call you again."

4

KEVIN PAUL

OFTEN I am asked why I do what I do. Since forensic anthropologists deal with death on a daily basis, I'm not always clear whether that question arises from the desire to know why a woman is in the field, or from curiosity about why anyone would choose a career that inevitably deals with the loss of human life and loved ones. Sometimes I answer that question with a brief story from the past.

I have always been drawn to puzzles, having spent many an hour of my youth putting together the cardboard kind with my five siblings. Puzzles, games of dominoes, card games like Crazy 8 and Rook, and the board game Monopoly often filled much of our spare time, especially during cold winters beside the fireplace. We took great pride in second-guessing which pieces of the puzzle to hoard to be "last piece in" or in trying to figure out just who held the ravenlike Rook super trump in games that seldom ended peacefully if the winner's top lip revealed any tooth past the canine. Of course, I became and remain a forensic anthropologist and bioarchaeologist for reasons much more complex than simply a childhood interest in solving puzzles and winning games.

I admit it. I am fascinated with death or, more precisely, with the rest of the story that continues after death. As I think back, way back, I realize how deep my fascination with the mysteries of death may be, not only as expressed in the bony elements of the human skeleton, but also in those intangible elements, not easily reconstructed like a group of bones, that lurk in the shadows of our psyche.

I believe my interest in death began at a very early time in my life, perhaps in the 1950s with my younger brother, Kevin Paul. We never called him just "Kevin"; it was always "Kevin Paul." Mama had lost three other sons prior to Kevin Paul, but he was the only one of those I knew. I was in second grade when he was born and was intrigued by his birth, having been banished with my older brother to the back porch where we listened in dread to the screams coming from Mama's room and stared in awe at the cloths our aunt continually piled into the old wringer washer by the back steps.

He was a beautiful baby, though a little blue in color, even to me. Some of his toes and fingers were webbed, a fact I admired greatly. I did not know that the webbing was a minor condition compared to the heart valve deformity that took his last breath on the operating table in Little Rock when he was less than a year old. Mama told us she and my father allowed the doctors to finish the surgery because it might save another child some day.

What I remember most about Kevin Paul's death was the day he was buried. He lay remotely in a small pink casket in the funeral home. Mama explained that it was the only child's casket the funeral director had on hand. Someone placed copper pennies on his eyes to keep them closed. I didn't like the pennies, but I didn't want his eyes to fly open during the service as Mama said they could.

Today, more than forty years later, when I receive a case that has the appearance of a disturbed cemetery burial rather than a recent forensic case for law enforcement, I routinely examine the remains for evidence of formal burial preparation. I check for bits of coffin lining and fabric, which sometimes cling to the bone. I look for tacks or pins that hold clothing in place. I search for small, convex, plastic disks in the eye sockets that morticians can place just under the eyelids. About the size of the iris, they give definition to the eye area when the person is lying supine and help to keep the eyelid closed. Occasionally, while doing so, I find myself also checking for copper pennies.

BENEATH THE CORN CRIB

A few years ago, a very pleasant lady arrived at my laboratory one afternoon carrying a small wooden box, approximately eighteen inches long. It was well constructed, hinged, and lined with velvet, probably pre–World War II, according to a textile expert I consulted later. The box was decorated on the outside with lambs in repose. One of the corner edges of the box had been gnawed away.

An intriguing part of this case is the fact that the box was discovered under the far end of a corn crib, or storage bin, in a barn that had been abandoned for more than fifty years. The barn was being torn down and the raised corn crib disassembled when the box came to light. The crib was only about a foot or so off the ground. In order for the box to have been positioned at the back of it, either someone very small had to have placed it there, or someone must have used a long object to push the box to the crib's farthermost corner.

Even more mysterious were the box's contents. Remnants of what could have been a military medal were found tucked within a small pile of debris, which resembled a mouse's nest. Only a frayed portion of the ribbon was left with a piece of a pin attached.

The woman who brought me the box had seen more than seventy summers fly by and could not recollect how such an item might have been left in her father's barn. Could a mouse have brought the medal in? Could someone have put the medal there, along with something else? Could an infant or fetus have been placed in the box, the fragile bones a source of nutrients for small animals? Or had someone performed a symbolic burial, the ribbon belonging to a fallen hero? Why didn't the person who hid the box under the crib bury it if something valued was inside? Or had the small container simply been used as a child's toy, the memory of it lost over time?

A couple of years later, I presented this case at a coroners' convention where many of the one hundred attendees were funeral home directors. My hope was that from their vast, collective experience of dealing with the dead, they could help with the mystery. As I flashed the slide of the small box upon the oversized viewing screen, I posed the question, "Does this look familiar to you?"

"Of course," they answered back in chorus.

"Mary, you have an infant's coffin there," one said. They all agreed, adding one small piece to a still-unsolved puzzle.

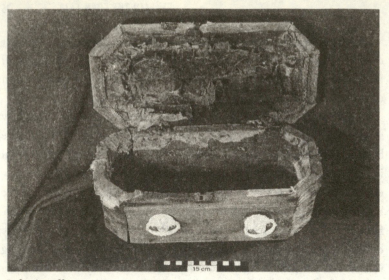

Infant's coffin

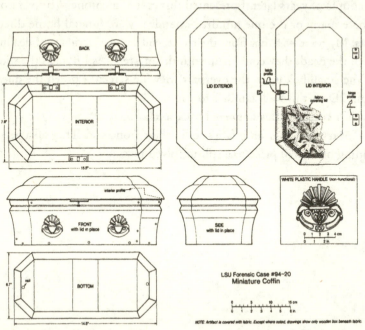

Scale drawings of infant's coffin

UNDER THE PORCH

THE phone rang early that morning back in 1991. To reach it, I pushed aside the alligator osteoderms recently delivered to my office as yet another unidentified "something." As they spilled across the desk, I mentally cataloged how much the small, circular bits of armorlike bone that run along a gator's back looked like ivory sand dollars.

"Mary, Bill Donovan, Jefferson Parish. There's a house, and a hollow front porch, and a metal door, and a skeleton. Can you come?"

Donovan, a coroner's investigator, and I had frequently worked together for several years. He was a man who wasted little time on greetings and salutations when requesting assistance in the sprawling parish that covered both the east and west banks of the Mississippi River. Well-educated and well-read, he could leisurely debate any topic for hours after work over a couple of beers in New Orleans's French Quarter. When on the clock, however, he tore around like a whirling dervish, absorbing every detail of a scene.

I gathered up a couple of graduate students and headed southeast.

As we rolled into the peaceful neighborhood with its row after row of small houses stacked closely, but neatly, together, the curious paved the way to the scene.

Donovan filled in the details of the case and I mentally put together a preliminary scenario for case number 91-17.

That morning, a termite inspector had crawled gingerly beneath the little cottage on Bennett Street. He was about to complete his requisite presale inspection. In the Deep South, the nasty little invaders have been known to eat their way into the heart of a building in a matter of months. Working his way toward the front of the house, the inspector pushed back a homemade metal grate covering the entryway to a hollow front porch. What he saw in the tomblike chamber interrupted and probably ruined his day. A human skeleton stared back at him from the dark, smelly recesses. His hasty retreat from under the house was slowed only by the beams on which he banged his head as he fled.

The pounding of jackhammers jarred me, their vibration rattling windows across the front of the house. The local police were cutting a hole through the outside wall of the concrete porch to create easy access to the body inside. The hole was just big enough for me to squeeze through and proved a little too close for my 6-foot, 2-inch assistant. His claustrophobia prevented him from lingering long at the entryway.

I pulled myself into the cool, darkened confines of the hollow porch and was at once reminded of Aunt Penny's storm cellar with its mason jars filled with vegetables and fruit sitting in long, orderly rows. I didn't really like being under the porch any more than in a clay cellar at midnight—rural North Louisiana's answer to the tornados that often hopscotch to and fro across the borders of the Ark-La-Tex.

I turned my attention to the case at hand. The skeleton lay across an old boxspring mattress, its wiry coils poking at my knees as I tried to get a closer look. Fully clothed, the body was supine, the cervical, or neck, vertebrae arching toward the ceiling of the chamber as though reaching toward heaven. I noted the clothing looked malelike, a preliminary assessment that is always subject to change.

"Dirt floor, rotting clothing, mainly bone, some mummified tissue," I called out to my assistant, who scribbled notes outside.

To the body I whispered, "What in the world are you doing here? And how are we going to get you out?"

My flashlight illuminated a gaping wound that had opened the right cheek bones and sent fractures radiating out across the skull. Probable bullet wound. Donovan brought in a portable metal detector to search for a gun, but the metal from the springs and other debris set off a continuous buzzing noise that bounced across the walls and back again creating a most annoying cacophony.

"Well, this won't do," Donovan noted. We had to get the person out of the tomb. The police officers filmed and photographed the removal as we worked, taking turns now and then to crawl out from under the porch for a breath of fresh air.

The rotting clothing on the skeleton assisted with the recovery effort. We gently rolled 91-17 into a hospital sheet, tucking the edges together like a shroud. Slowly we moved the body through the opening and into the light. There, I could see small amounts of adipocere clinging to some of the bone. Parts of the skeleton were a golden brown. It had been in this death chamber for quite some time. There was no smell of decay, just the damp, earthy odor of something old sliding into my senses.

I finished recovering small pieces of evidence from the crowded space beneath the little porch on Bennett Street: glassware, ceramics, a candle, bits of a broken mirror. Inside the clothing law enforcement personnel found a billfold, a few coins, and a set of keys. Then as carefully as possible, we loaded the fragile skeleton into the black vinyl body bag for the trip to my lab. The coroner's office had released the case into my care.

Back at the lab, we laid the remains on the X-ray table, leaving the rotting clothing intact for the first radiographs. Preliminary X rays often can aid in trauma assessment, especially when we are looking for bullet fragments. The X-ray room, our pride and joy, had been designed and built for us when the new addition to the Geology Building was completed in 1987. Over the years I had filled it with diagnostic equipment purchased with grants and private donations. Though our X-ray machine is housed in a lead-lined room, nuclear safety personnel routinely monitor our equipment and procedures.

Guided by years of experience in determining precise equipment settings to ensure clear, crisp X rays for any type of case—full body tissue or otherwise—I set the machine for dry bone. The radiographs of the skull pinpointed tiny bits of metal lodged in the right cheek bones. An exit wound on the left lower jaw provided corroboration that a gunshot had entered the right side of the face. The bullet had then sliced through an upper dental plate, missed the braincase, and exited the skull in a downward trajectory through the left mandible. The wound might not have been immediately fatal: death might have been slow and painful.

After taking the X rays, we eased the case onto the examining table. The lack of soft tissue precluded further preparation before skeletal analysis. Hair still clung to small bits of dried scalp tissue, its neat, uniform length suggesting a well-groomed head. The hip bones, corresponding to the male human model, poked through the rotting cloth. They were fused to the sacrum, a condition occasionally seen in older individuals. The skeleton exhibited arthritic changes in most of the other joints, and the bones were lightweight and porous. The shoulder blade was almost transparent. The aging process had not been kind to 91-17.

He did indeed fit the profile of the man whose name was recorded on a driver's license found in the billfold: Cornelius Harmon, white male, age seventy-two years.

I thought about his life but found it difficult to reconstruct his story. The police records noted that he was known to be a happy man. "His neighbors remembered a kind, aging face, always smiling," one document read. "He often chatted with the neighborhood children, his gold tooth a characteristic they recalled with fondness."

"Why did it have to end this way?" I thought.

The coroner's office—the agency that issues all death certificates for a particular parish—called a few days later and informed me that most likely 91-17 was the former resident of the house on Bennett Street, a conclusion confirmed in part by our profile, the shiny gold tooth that was attached to his dental plate, and the personal effects from his pocket. Old police day records revealed that his car had been found abandoned several blocks from his home years before; it was thought at the time that he had met with foul play.

Harmon left home one Sunday afternoon as usual but never arrived for his weekly visit with relatives who lived two hours away by car. For seventeen years he lay there in his secret place, a safe place, the place that became his self-made tomb. During many of those years, his wife and son went about their normal routine in the rooms above. Further recovery work revealed that his personal handgun rested at his side.

THE ROSE GARDEN

ON a cold March day I stood at the side of Antoine Hebert's former house on Lutcher Street, staring down at the skeletal remains of his first wife wrapped in the frayed remnants of a polyester mattress cover. Hand bones protruded from beneath its ragged edges. As I leaned over to clean away the water-soaked soil, a diamond from a set of wedding rings caught the sun's rays and brought a slight gasp and whistle from one of the officers assisting me. A perimortem break—one that occurs at or near the time of death—in one of the small metacarpals of the left hand suggested a struggle. Colleen Hebert's parents already knew their daughter was not coming home. Now they would have a few more remains to bury.

Colleen's fractured skull and other bones had arrived at my laboratory a few days before, and positive identification using dental records came from Doctors Barsley and Carr a short while later.

Eight years before Colleen had just up and disappeared one night. Antoine swore she had run away with another man. He later produced an affidavit from a friend of his saying the friend had seen her in a local mall. Her parents thought differently. They knew Colleen dearly loved her two small daughters and swore she would never have left them for anyone. They suspected that harm had come to Colleen.

Lead after lead went nowhere. Colleen's parents grieved over the disappearance of their daughter. Meanwhile, Antoine Hebert would talk to the mirror in the bathroom at the house on Lutcher Street. When the window was open, one could smell the roses in the garden just outside. Late one night his second wife, Jolie, heard him call out to Colleen, telling her how great supper had been and what a good cook she was.

The rose garden and concrete pad Antoine had placed alongside the house had never attracted much attention. He had always puttered in the yard. No one knew that beneath the rose garden lay Colleen's battered body.

Antoine sold the red brick house on Lutcher Street in a cash sale to an elderly lady. Life might have gone OK for him except for one thing. The elderly lady up and sold the house to a young couple whose lending agency required that a new septic tank be installed for sewage disposal. Before the tank could be lowered into place, a drainage trench, or filter bed, had to be made.

The backhoe dug the drainage trench right down the side of the house on Lutcher Street, right through the rose garden, and right through the grave of Colleen. By that time, Antoine and Jolie were divorced, and she would later testify in court to his strange bathroom conversations.

The week-long trial drew standing-room-only crowds, spectators spilling out into the hallways and onto the courthouse square. During extensive cross-examination, the defense attorney grilled me on retrieval techniques and minute details of Colleen's fractured remains. He wanted to convince the jury that her broken bones could have resulted from the backhoe activities when the sewage trench was being dug and when we recovered the rest of her body that cold March day. However, Colleen's bones told her story. The perimortem fractures on her skeleton were distinguished from the postmortem injuries by the staining on the older trauma and the sharp, warped edges of once-vital, living bone that had been displaced violently. The recent trauma caused by the backhoe exposed dry and whitened edges of brittle bone that had long lost its resiliency and ability to resist stress.

Near the end of the last day, the defense attorney had only one more expert witness to challenge: Dr. Alfredo Suarez, a no-nonsense, cigar-smoking, South American Houdini with a scalpel and one of the best forensic pathologists with whom I have ever worked.

Succinct as ever, especially when pressed, Suarez merely had to take the stand, point to the gaping perimortem wound in the back of Colleen's skull, and say, "See that hole? Ain't s'posed to be there."

Conviction; life without parole.

AMONG THE SHADOWS

I N my first semester of graduate school, I was especially inspired by Doug Owsley, a new professor at LSU at the time. Volunteering to work in his bone lab led to an assistantship there, where I put together human skeletal puzzles. Doug and I tackled many projects together before he left the university in 1987 to accept a nonacademic position in physical anthropology at the Museum of Natural History, the Smithsonian Institution. Today he often works with war crimes recovery teams and spearheads efforts to preserve ancient human remains for scientific study.

One of our largest projects together began in 1986 when we contracted to excavate a cemetery in New Orleans that had been discovered during a street-renewal project. While skimming the upper two feet of Canal Boulevard at Metairie Road, construction workers uncovered what is often referred to as the Cypress Grove II/Charity Hospital Cemetery. Though records are somewhat ambiguous about its past, it was established in the 1840s. From then until the 1920s, thousands of people were buried in the cemetery. Fifteen days of retrieval efforts resulted in the recovery of more than 250 historic burials, many of which contained pathologies and trauma. The bones told stories of the city's past, and the archival records revealed a harsh but colorful history.

Various accounts reflected a matter-of-fact attitude about death and a nonchalance for corpses that in many circles today would seem irreverent. Since New Orleans is below sea level, reports of floating coffins following heavy rainstorms were not that uncommon. Citizens worried about "miasmic" odors arising from the cemetery, where children could be seen occasionally kicking skulls back and forth for amusement while passing that way.

We discovered burials that reflected the cross section of an exotic, yet difficult life: a bullet wound to the back where the lead was still lodged in the remodeled bone, an indication that the person had lived for a considerable time after the wound had occurred (my students swear to this day that it must have been a duel); a poorly healed, bilateral break in both thigh bones of a young adult (possibly the result of falling from a rooftop or being run over by a wagon); a dog buried with a human (maybe his master); two persons in one coffin (a slight matter of economy); and many bones covered with cut marks representing multiple persons who were buried in several long, rectangular boxes. Scalpel handles and other medical debris in the boxes suggested they came from one of the old medical schools, perhaps where medical students were practicing their amputation skills. Amputation was the rule rather than the exception as a response to infection in the nineteenth century. At that time, knowledge of disease was scarce, and yellow fever, smallpox, and cholera killed thousands in New Orleans alone.

In the 1980s, protection and preservation of rediscovered cemeteries depended a lot upon public outcry when news spread throughout a community that old cemeteries were being disturbed and destroyed. Tight construction schedules often played a role in complicating these preservation efforts. As of 1992 an "unmarked burials" law in Louisiana protects such sites.

Today New Orleans, like many cities, still has remnants of historic cemeteries in unsuspected places, and daily people are surrounded by the dead. It could well be that the Superdome's close proximity to one such burial site, old Girod Street Cemetery, explains the thirty-five-year history of New Orleans's football team, the Saints.

One of my fondest memories of working with Doug Owsley involves the power of storytelling. During the winter of 1986–1987 we took a long road trip with Murray Marks, Doug's former research associate, now a professor of physical anthropology at the University of Tennessee in Knoxville—home of the famous "body farm."* As Doug's assistants, we were helping to assess all human skeletal material in museums throughout the southwest. One night in Norman, Oklahoma, at the Stovall Museum stands out from the others during that whirlwind trip.

As usual, we were working late—Doug with eagerness, Murray and I with something less, given the hour—in order to complete a project. We were surrounded by archival materials on the museum's top floor: for company we had human skeletal remains, mastodons, and other extinct animals shrouded in canvas and plaster covers. Apart from us the museum and campus were deserted.

Perhaps inspired by our work and the late hour and our isolation, I began telling a story featuring an older gentleman I met earlier in the

---

*The Forensic Anthropology Laboratory at the University of Tennessee at Knoxville has an outdoor research facility where human bodies are exposed on the surface in order for scientists to monitor their various rates of decay. This facility is often referred to in the press as the "body farm."

day who had inquired about our project. Sitting in a corner, Murray, a great trickster, helped me spin the tale—in voices audible to Doug—of the gentleman's "early retirement" from the museum where he had worked as a curator. We could tell that Doug was listening. The gentleman, we observed, had also worked late into the night. His career in the lab had been uneventful . . . that is, until just prior to his sudden departure from the museum staff.

"It seems," I related, "that an experience here forced him to leave. He had come to know and love this museum: to him, despite its loneliness, it felt comfortable, like home. Then late one evening while working in the stacks, he looked down the corridor and caught a glimpse of a doglike animal dragging one leg."

This last touch was inspired by a sudden recollection of my Aunt Penny's story about a wolflike creature who haunted the rise just above a swimming hole not too far from our home in Northwest Louisiana. I know now that her story was intended to keep us children out of the pond, since we could not swim, when we struck out for the woods nearby. And I know, too, that this creature, whom some call the *loup-garou,* figures prominently in Louisiana folklore.

"The curator," I continued, "was frightened but said nothing. Then just as suddenly as it appeared, the animal was gone. But the curator could not forget it. Shaken, he avoided working at night and soon retired."

"What happened after that?" Murray prompted.

"He never saw the creature again," I said, "but he thought it was a sign." No sooner had I uttered those words than the old building emitted a creak, immediately capturing Doug's attention, as well as the storytellers'. Then Murray and I began to howl with laughter.

The last laugh, however, was on me. We had drunk so much tea earlier in the evening that a trip to the restroom, located on the museum's first floor, now became imperative. And I had no idea where that floor's light switch might be. The prospect of descending into total darkness was too much for me: I had told the dog-goblin story too well. Only when Doug decided to call it quits for the evening did we all go downstairs together, each of us, I think, watching for glowing eyes in the shadows. Murray and I never told Doug we made up the whole thing.

IN THE WOODS

DOUG OWSLEY inspired me during my early years in the field, but it was Ann Marie Mires, one of his former research associates, who guided me. In 1997 Dr. Mires became Director of the Human Identification Unit for the Office of the State Medical Examiner in Boston, Massachusetts.

Many years ago on a cold and windy day—rare in Louisiana—Ann Marie called me at home. She was then a recent Connecticut transplant, about as big as a minute, and one of the funniest people I have ever met; I was a graduate student in my second year.

"We have a case!" she said. "Put on your long johns; it's a field recovery." At that point in our careers, neither of us had yet had a forensic case in which we could utilize our archaeological skills, skills I had honed in cemetery excavations and that Ann Marie had perfected at the University of Arkansas with Dr. Jerome Rose.

We met at the laboratory and planned our strategy. Our simple field kit included four small wooden stakes with pointed ends to set up an archaeological square surrounding the scene; string to enclose and protect the square at ground level; a line level to assist in measuring depth below surface; a compass to plot our coordinates; shovels and trowels; four metric tapes; graph paper to draw our site map on; plastic bags to hold evidence; waterproof pens; a hand-held screen for searching for small pieces of evidence; and the requisite black vinyl body bag. The condition of the body was unknown.

Arriving at the scene, we were met by law enforcement personnel and news media. As we stepped past the media with straight faces, while trying to make our way into the woods, Ann Marie advised softly, "Look serious, no matter what."

Oftentimes the media will capture us in the oddest of poses, and the seriousness of what we do can be misconstrued by isolated footage used outside of its context. Years later, at another field recovery, I became acutely aware of the value of Ann Marie's advice. We had emerged from the field carrying a body bag when one television reporter, in an attempt to have "first coverage," began slipping and sliding in the mud ahead of us and almost ended up on his bottom. Of course, I broke down into laughter, and, of course, that was the film clip shown on another television station that evening.

The body lay before us in the lightly wooded area. A few inches of debris covered the skeleton. No soft tissue was left, just bone. The skull, minus the mandible, lay off to one side. Law enforcement personnel wanted our opinion on whether or not the case was a deliberate burial or whether environmental factors had contributed to obscuring the remains.

In Louisiana, decomposition of a body exposed to the elements proceeds very quickly, especially in warm weather. Hair can separate from the head in a mass two days after death. Some teeth, especially the upper and lower front teeth, can fall out in just as short a time. In two weeks, a body can be reduced to bone and a few tendinous attachments.

Our initial survey of the site, the first step in our protocol before proceeding with anything else, resolved the burial issue. The region was low; water stains clearly marked the surrounding saplings. These stains indicated that the area most likely flooded periodically, bringing leaves, twigs, and other lightweight flora up and around the body. It lay below the debris but was not buried.

Our preliminary assessment also revealed that the entire skeleton was bleached and dry, producing a mottled appearance similar in color to the gray and white Spanish moss that hung from the surrounding trees. I would come to know that color well over the next fifteen years. Small plants had woven themselves in and out among the remains. The bleached bone was what had drawn the man who found the remains to the site in the first place. He had been walking in the wooded area and had spotted it from a distance. Frightened, he called police, and they took it from there.

The clothing provided other clues about case number 83-20. In Louisiana, natural fibers such as cotton, silk, and linen can deteriorate very quickly. Thick cotton jeans can be reduced to wads of thread and a zipper in just six months when left unprotected on the earth's surface. On the other hand, synthetic fibers such as polyester can last for many years, a legacy from the 1970s. The clothing on our case was somewhat intact. The label in the sweater collar suggested why: "100% polyester; wash in warm water."

We set out our tapes and began the arduous task of slowly mapping the position of the body and all surrounding artifacts. "Artifact" is an archaeological term that has been adopted by forensic scientists. Literally, it means "anything that was altered or used by man" and can include even the trauma to a body, such as a bullet hole, which could be an "artifact" of death. Our map, or plan view, would provide a drawing of the exact position of the body as though seen from above.

The body rested on its back. The left leg was bent, the right leg straight. The shoes still contained the socks, and foot bones could be seen inside. Most of the body lay in its original position. Animals had not moved many of the remains.

The skull told the story: an entry wound to the left temple, a much larger exit wound to the right side of the head. A gun and box of un-used bullets lay close by, clearly defined once we were allowed to clean away the debris.

We finished mapping the site, placing all the remains in a body bag for the trip to our lab. There we began the familiar process of skeletal analysis. Ann Marie's patient style and careful eye for detail had taught me well in our brief time together. Many years later I would recall how easily we handled such cases as a team at a time when the field was dominated by men. Now in the late 1990s at least as many women as men enter the profession of forensic anthropology—maybe even more.

The case from the woods was a female, reported missing some five years earlier. The coroner in that parish ruled it a suicide. The gun's serial number assisted in tracing the weapon to a shop where the woman had purchased it the night she disappeared.

In a magnanimous gesture, her family donated her skeleton to our FACES Laboratory to be held in perpetuity as a teaching aid for train-ing graduate students in forensic anthropology. Over the years, several families have made similar donations, for which we are most grateful.

THE CAST-IRON COFFIN

OVER the years, my friends have often asked if I ever felt spooked when dealing with someone's bones. "Usually not," I say. But sometimes I go on to tell the story of the "Spaniard."

In the Plains, a small community just outside Zachary, Louisiana, lies the Young family cemetery, just down the road from where I lived in the 1980s. Near this private cemetery, at a little country store where I often stopped for milk, former store owner David Mills would tell the story about a cast-iron coffin and a "Spaniard" who was buried in the cemetery. I knew from my research that Spanish land grants had occurred throughout the region. The prospect of examining a "lost" Spaniard who had ended up in the Young family cemetery was too intriguing to dismiss.

During the 1960s, while preparing a grave site for one of his family members, David Mills and his workmen hit something that looked like a metal pipe, thinking it part of an unknown pipeline running through the cemetery. Additional soil removal, however, revealed a cast-iron coffin protruding from the wall of the freshly dug grave. Meticulous records contained no reference to a burial in that region of the cemetery. Mills decided to remove the coffin to try to get to the bottom of the mystery; besides, the deceased family member was waiting to be interred there that day.

He placed the coffin in his garage for a few days, during which time he noticed a metal plate attached with screws at the head region. He realized that beneath that plate was probably a piece of glass, the viewing window. It was common for cast-iron coffins from the 1700s and 1800s to contain such a window, allowing families to see the face of their loved one prior to burial. Sealed in quiet repose, the person remained lifelike without having undergone the now common routine of embalming.

Mills removed the metal plate to peer into the past. "I was shocked," he recalled. "I saw what I thought was a Spaniard. He had a beard, was dark skinned, and wore a ruffled shirt. He was perfectly preserved." Perplexed but determined to show proper respect for the dead, Mills reburied the "Spanish" gentleman at the front of the cemetery in a shallow grave and often recounted the story to patrons at the store he visited daily.

When Mills told me the story, I had visions of an eighteenth-century burial. Generally, preservation of human remains in Louisiana is poor. Our subtropic climate—including heavy rainfalls, long hot summers, and locally acidic soil—greatly accelerate the normal decomposition process of buried bodies. Unlike some regions of the United States where drier conditions can help in preserving human remains, most old burials in Louisiana have turned to dust in a hundred years. Cast-iron coffin burials are sometimes exceptions.

Because a great deal of historical and biological information could be gained from looking at someone who might be very old and whose tissue might be preserved, I asked Doug Owsley in 1987 if he would be interested in pursuing this project with me. He agreed. The "perpetual caretakers" for the Young family cemetery—including one of their historians, Drew Burk—allowed us to recover the cast-iron coffin and take it to our laboratory at LSU.

The coffin was large and quite heavy. As we removed it from the ground, we noted that one side was damaged; a small hole had rusted through. However, dirt plugged the hole, and we hoped for some preservation of the body. At the cemetery, the metal face cover was removed for the second time in twenty years for family members to see inside.

The crowd that had gathered pushed forward, both young and old resting on their knees to press their faces against the glass and look into the darkened recesses. With a flashlight, one could see that though the skull had shifted somewhat, some of the body remained intact.

We transported the coffin to our laboratory at LSU and placed it at the back where we prepared bones for analysis. Occasionally, I would take the flashlight and try to see inside. I was intrigued by the man in the coffin.

I worked in the lab on a daily basis, and my back was usually turned to the coffin, which rested on the floor against the wall and whose mysterious man waited inside. I often worked alone, cleaning bone, and much of my work allowed my mind to wander. Lost in daydreams one day yet cognizant of the coffin behind me, I heard a loud noise that came from the corner where the "Spaniard" lay. For one brief moment I mustered all the courage I had to face the coffin. Swallowing hard, I finally turned—expecting what, I don't know. As an avid horror movie fan during my younger years in Shreveport, I spent Saturday afternoons at the Joy Theater. There, the dimes I had squirreled away introduced me to the likes of Boris Karloff's Mummy and Lon Chaney, Jr.'s Wolfman. I had not lost the ability to experience chills up and down my spine. On this occasion, though, the cause proved to be simply a large chunk of hard dirt falling from the side of the coffin with that deafening thud.

Eventually, the cast-iron coffin was transported to the Smithsonian Institution. I was present there for the opening, which brought great fanfare and public attention as well as a few turned-up noses from the smell. For me, the final opening at the Smithsonian was anticlimactic. Death for the white, middle-aged male had clearly postdated the 1850s; his clothing had been machine-stitched. In fact, further research indicated that, most likely, he was a Young family member buried in the cemetery following the end of the Civil War, his death record lost in the war's aftermath.

FIRE IN THE SKY

ON a hot and humid August day, "field recovery" in one of Louisiana's industrial plants took on a new meaning for me. A raging fire had raced through a section of the plant and filled the sky with flames and smoke.

Calls from private industry usually come a day or so after the explosions and fires. First, the plant safety personnel try to find the bodies of the missing workers with little outside help. Then they call. The fires burn quick and hot in these plants, sometimes going for days before burning out completely. It's only when the cooling begins and the steam and process gas lines are stable that, even suited in special gear, we are permitted to enter an operating unit.

The plants always look the same, and so do the people. The blackened, deformed, melted structures are but backdrops for the shock, worry, and relief on the workers' faces. They stare curiously back at you as you file past them heading for the briefing room and the inevitable, ill-fitting gear. OSHA (Occupational Safety and Health Administration) regulations run long and hard. We constantly rinse and rerinse our boots, and, like quick-change artists, strip off and replace disposable jumpsuits as we go.

My arrival at the plant on that August day drew hushed murmurs from the crowd. As I surveyed the carnage from the entry gate, I saw it had been an especially bad fire. Once the fire had been put out, two persons were found and tentatively identified; one man remained missing. Plant safety personnel had narrowed down to two the most likely places where the man's body might be: either deep in one of the storage vats on the ground or high on a burned-out tower some sixty feet tall.

After suiting up, we slowly made our way to the burned-out unit, the acrid smell of smoldering buildings and the sweet odor of strange chemicals mixing in the air. As we neared the center zone, I saw the tower in front of me, its water-soaked base a maze of debris. "Where do you think the body might be?"asked the exhausted young man standing near me. With a slight shrug of my shoulders, I took in the mass of twisted, burned, and blackened structures. My heart sank. This recovery would take a lot longer than the afternoon I had hoped to give.

I looked at the twisted tower. I looked at the vat. I looked at my assistant, then I swallowed hard. I would climb the tower while he would head for the vat, I decided. The look on his face silently thanked me for not sending him up the shaky, skeletonlike structure.

The safety personnel and I carefully climbed the tower, crisscrossing back and forth between catwalks to reach our goal. At one corner edge of the third level, we saw remnants of goggles and a safety shield. Had they belonged to the missing man? Their generic nature did not provide an answer. I glanced down below wondering if the man had dived into the vat into whose depths my assistant now stood looking.

We climbed down from the tower with plans to return if necessary, provided a catwalk to the distant edge could be stabilized.

Smelly, sticky goo smoldered in the vat as the bucket in which I was riding swung back and forth across the area, sweeping the perimeter. Most of the ten-foot layer of surface water in the vat had been removed. The brownish-black, viscous material that was left bubbled here and there as air made its way to the surface, reminding me of the shallow pools of natural asphalt in the LaBrea tar pits of Los Angeles. Nothing yet found on the tower; nothing in the vat. I gave the thumbs-up gesture for the machine operator to haul me back to solid ground and prepared reluctantly to leave the plant that day. While I worked to obtain positive identifications on the first two victims, my assistant would remain on site with instructions to call at the first sign of human remains. As twilight approached, I somehow knew the sun would rise again before we had any news to give the young man's family, who would doubtless be holding the age-old vigil.

The plant workers were on the tower the next morning when they found him. He had fallen between two large elevated storage tanks in an area inaccessible to us the day before. Once again I had to climb the tower. The new routes we took reminded me of the switchbacks I would be walking high in the Colorado mountains a few days from then. I had been preparing for my hiking and camping trip for months by taking ten-mile walks without stopping and pumping gallon milk bottles filled with water to build my upper-body strength. The fifty pounds of gear I would be packing on my back would get lighter during the week only by the subtraction of food I ate each day.

When we reached the third level, the plant workers hooked a lifeline to our safety harness to ensure that we would not end up in the vat. We crossed the ledge, rounded the corner, and then I saw him, lying between the two tanks. As a deputy coroner, I had the authority to declare the victim dead. Declaring him dead was one thing; getting him back to earth was another. I glanced down into the depths of the storage tank, the sixty-foot drop looking much greater from above.

I found the heat was almost unbearable wearing three layers of clothes: my own shorts and shirt, the plant's oversized coveralls, and the disposable jumpsuit. Added to that were a helmet and mask, gloves and goggles. Nevertheless, I foolishly dived right in. It did not matter that men had been dropping like flies in the heat all day—I was macho woman in training for the mountains.

I was leaning over, fast and furiously removing the debris from around the victim's body. In the distance, a storm cloud moved steadily toward the plant. We were told we had only a short time left before we had to clear the tower for safety reasons.

Then it snuck up on me, like some insidious dream snake wrapping its long body around me and squeezing my chest. It began with my mask. The steam given off by the insulation material covering the victim filled my mask with moisture and no air could penetrate the fibers.

I straightened up, suddenly feeling wobbly, knowing I had to get back across the narrow ledge or risk passing out as I went. I recall my voice coming from outside of me when I spoke to whoever was close by: "I can't breathe. Get me out of here. I'm going out. Water . . . get me water, and a new face mask."

I know I scared them. I scared myself.

Unfortunately, supplies were located on the next level down. I looked out across the distance and I felt the world going black. All I could think of was that I had never seen Colorado's Rocky Mountains—a high priority on my "to-do" list after recent cancer surgery—and that I would not make it there after all.

"Breathe, Miss Mary, breathe," I heard someone say. But I just didn't want to anymore. Passing out was like a gentle release, a gradual sinking into nothingness.

"Is this what it's like to die?" I wondered, never having passed out before.

Then the safety personnel began stripping me, high on the tower that day in the August heat. "Miss Mary, Miss Mary, can we take off your coveralls?"

"Sure, take them," I vaguely replied.

"Can we take off your T-shirt?" they asked.

"Of course, of course," I murmured, only half-aware that somewhere on a mangled and burned-out tower in a place that was as hot as hell, I was in the process of being relieved of my dignity . . . and that it didn't matter one little bit.

"What about your pants?" they hollered at me.

"What about my pants?" I tried to reason. What did my pants have to do with breathing?

At just about that time, a splash of cold water hit me, pouring over my head and down my face like a mountain stream. Nothing ever felt so good. I came back from wherever I was, the only woman high on a tower, surrounded by worried faces anxiously watching me, awkwardly helping to reassemble my clothing and gear. I sat there for a few minutes, contemplating my situation. I drank a bottle or two of something and had my pulse checked by safety personnel who voiced obvious relief at my rapid recovery. Then I went back to work.

Ten minutes later we lowered the body in a basket to the hearse that was waiting below.

I climbed down from the tower that day feeling a little self-conscious, now that the guys had seen me half-undressed, but not minus my pants. Yet, as I cautiously made my way down the twisted trail, I also felt relieved knowing that, after this experience, I could handle Colorado's mountains with ease. As I exited the plant checkout booth, one of the workers leaned over for just a moment and confided, "No disrespect, ma'am, but I always was a sucker for a lady in a lace bra."

I simply laughed and walked away, glad to be able to do so.

LOST AND MISSING CHILDREN

IN any death case, whether it is a child or an adult, assessing cause of death is a necessary part of the examination process. Cause of death refers to the action or condition that results in death and can include such things as drowning, a blow to a vital region, a heart attack, a stroke, or a sharp-instrument wound if there is soft tissue to examine. A medical doctor, usually a board-certified pathologist, makes the final determination.

If very little tissue remains on the body or if only bone is available for examination, forensic anthropologists are often consulted. We carefully study each of the bones, often under a binocular scope. Among other things, we look for such evidence as blunt force fractures to the skull, gunshot trauma to the head or chest, a sharp-instrument wound or blunt trauma to a rib, or, perhaps, pressure fractures to the hyoid, the small bone in the neck. The hyoid looks a little like a miniature horseshoe and helps to anchor the tongue in place. It can be damaged during strangulation; however, it starts out in three pieces—the center part, or body, and two major wings, or horns. The horns often fuse to the body of the hyoid by a person's mid-thirties, but they also may never fuse. Particular caution should be taken when examining this important piece of evidence because it may be unfused rather than broken. Unfortunately, it is not often recovered when remains have been scattered.

In contrast to cause of death, manner of death refers to whether the death is a result of natural or unknown causes, homicide, suicide, or accident. Typically, neither cause of death nor manner of death falls within the legal purview of forensic anthropologists, but we are able to describe what we see. These descriptions can aid forensic pathologists, law enforcement officials, and juries.

Though adult skeletons constitute the largest percentage of my yearly case load, occasionally I am asked to examine the remains of children. Every case that comes through the FACES Laboratory affects me, but the remains of children that end up there are, without question, the hardest cases to accept. They sometimes challenge my ability to maintain the neutral, unbiased facade that I ordinarily adopt with my cases and are grim reminders that even children sometimes cannot escape an untimely, and often unnatural, death.

In many of our typical cases, cause of death can be readily assessed in the adult skeleton. The same is not true for children's skeletons. Beginning in utero, a child has more than 800 growth areas, which eventually form the bony skeleton. At birth, the number has been reduced to just over 400 bones and epiphyses. These bones are still developing and are easily damaged. By adulthood, when growth is complete and most of the major epiphyses have fused, the number of bones has been further reduced to 206.

A child's skeleton is very easy to damage. Minor injuries to the bone often suffered during accidents or from abuse may remodel in the rapid growth phase and may not be as noticeable as the child matures.

In 1988 a coroner's investigator called me one day and announced, "We are bringing you some skeletal remains of what we believe to be a small child, around the age of two years. Could you confirm that profile and look for cause of death?"

The remains of the young child were pitifully few. Her body had lain in the woods for weeks, and no tissue was left on the fragile bones, only a strong odor of putrefaction. I referred to 88-10 as "she" because the officers knew that a female child was missing; however, I could not tell for certain if the remains were those of a male or female. Sexing the remains of young children is difficult because the bones of males and females look very similar to one another. Around eleven to thirteen years, that is, at the onset of puberty, the major morphological differences between the sexes begin to show in the bones, especially in the hips. Though some research supports sexing of immature skeletons, assigning sex in small children is risky and can be counterproductive in the end. Since sex determination is part of the major profile of a case, getting it wrong prematurely can delay the resolution of identification.

I began my analysis by X-raying the skull, especially noting the stages to which the teeth had developed. The most accurate age indicator for a child through eighteen years is tooth development. As mammals, we have two sets of teeth. Our first set, our baby, or deciduous teeth, number 20: 8 incisors, 4 canines, and 8 molars. These first teeth are replaced by 32 permanent teeth: 8 incisors, 4 canines, 8 premolars, and 12 molars. Often dentists refer to the canines and premolars as cuspids and bicuspids, respectively. The canines have one cusp, or raised ridge, on the biting surface and the premolars have two.

Generally, the growth and development of teeth are not as severely impacted by diet and other external factors as the rest of the skeletal system can be. While lack of a proper diet can stunt growth of long bones, teeth seem to be more genetically controlled. Teeth grow from the crown down to the root rather than from the root up to the crown, and that growth can be evaluated for age. If a child's twelve-year molars, the second permanent molars in his molar row, have erupted, I can suggest that he is probably between the ages of ten and twelve years. Forensic anthropologists always provide an age range because skeletal age and chronological age may differ slightly.

Case 88-10 had a set of baby teeth equivalent to that of a two-year-old child. The deciduous molars were nearly completely formed, their roots clearly visible on a lateral X ray. Though some of the other teeth had fallen out in the woods and were missing, the sharp-edged crypts, or sockets, documented their former presence.

I looked for clues to her past, including signs of previous abuse: a broken or healed rib; a fractured skull, leg, or arm bone; and remodeling of muscle attachment sites that might suggest chronic stress at a young age. Her hyoid was not found. The only thing that seemed a little out of the ordinary was the left tibia. The left and right tibiae, the larger of the lower leg bones, looked different from one another. At its proximal, or top end, near where the kneecap, or patella, fits, I could see a slight swelling in the left one. The asymmetry between the two sides became more apparent with an X ray.

However, consultation with the director of Children's Services for the state, a pediatrician, provided no further diagnosis. Though additional research suggested that such swelling might indicate trauma, that trauma simply could have resulted from an accidental fall. The mother of the missing female child said her daughter had died of natural causes, and she had become scared, wrapped the body in a blanket, and placed it in the woods. We were at a dead end. Authorities had no evidence to pursue the case. The case was closed. However, it inspired one of our graduate students in forensic anthropology to complete a master's thesis on evidence of abuse in the skeletons of children.

Though such cases as the little girl in the woods are never forgotten, our immediate attention must focus on others that follow. In 1992 a flattened mass of desiccated tissue and broken bones came to my laboratory. An X ray confirmed that the remains were all that was left of a human fetus. The fractured arm bones and hands of the baby revealed it to be about five months or so into development. I established the age by measuring the length of the metacarpals, the first row of tubular bones in the hand. I then used a growth chart to suggest an age range from the bones' length.

The remains were found in a plastic bag next to a trash dumpster and had been there for at least two months. No other information about the identity of the fetus was ever found.

One particularly hard juvenile case from 1994 involved a child whose remains came to my laboratory following autopsy. The difficulty arose when the pathologist and I disagreed about what had fractured the child's skull. The doctor was of the opinion that the fractures were caused by a gunshot wound. In my opinion, and in my court testimony at the trial of the accused, the fractures were produced by blunt force. The telltale fracture pattern was clearly visible once the skull was reconstructed, though the warping impeded the reconstruction process.

In such a case, where differences in opinion arise, I encourage authorities to consult with other experts. Another forensic anthropologist corroborated my opinion: "Massive blunt force trauma to the skull," he said; "at least two, maybe three blows."

I find a statement attributed to Dr. Clyde Snow, internationally renowned forensic anthropologist, useful to remember when my analysis is at odds with another expert: "Bones don't lie; you just have to understand what they are telling you." Of course, the only one who really knows what happened to the child is in prison now, on death row, awaiting his appeal.

For those children who enter our laboratory in boxes or in bags, there is no hope; for those who are missing and unaccounted for, hope drives us steadily, though warily, toward our goal—finding them alive. Few jobs evoke such strong emotion as the search for missing children. Though all such searches do not have happy endings, some do.

In 1985 Congress established the National Center for Missing and

Exploited Children (NCMEC). Associated with the National Center, based in Virginia, are Model Age Progression Sites, referred to as "MAPS." As of January 1999, fewer than ten of these sites exist. Most of them are located in law enforcement agencies or in the offices of the states attorneys general. Only one such site in the country is located within a university. In 1994 Eileen Barrow and I were able to work with the National Center to create a MAP site at Louisiana State University. Having the Missing and Exploited Children's Clearinghouse for our state associated with our Office of Children's Services in Baton Rouge also assisted greatly with LSU's designation as a MAPS location. Assistance from MAPS at LSU is one of the services we offer under the FACES Laboratory.

Since 1995 we have one certified age progression specialist on staff, Eileen Barrow. During the first three years of operation, our lab was able to assist with reuniting two children with their families.

NCMEC has provided the FACES Laboratory with software, called "Photosketch," for aging children and adults and has updated it several times. To complete an age progression on a child, we need some essential items: a photograph of the child at the age the child went missing and photographs of both parents at the age to which we need to progress the child. For example, if a child disappears at age ten and has been missing for five years, then we need photographs of both parents at age fifteen, or as close to that age as possible. Generally, the age progression specialist begins with the photo of the parent whom the child most closely resembles. That parent's photo eventually is merged through a grid system with the child's photo. To supplement the result and depict the child in contemporary clothing, the specialist selects features from a database composed of anonymous children's photographs. Teeth, hairdos, and clothing are examples of features pulled from this database.

This same software can be used to age adults. For age progressions on adults, parents' photographs are not needed, though they can be helpful if available. In 1997 an age progression of an adult developed at our MAP site was used by the FBI to apprehend a missing felon who had been on the lam for more than twenty years.

Through our contact with NCMEC, Eileen and I gathered information on a community action program sponsored by the U.S. Justice Department. Cities that participate in this program become "sites" of the Missing and Exploited Children's Comprehensive Action Program (M/CAP). Twenty-three of these M/CAP sites currently exist across the country. They foster communication among the various local agencies that deal with children. The federal government sponsors training for this program free of charge. Through the initial work of the LSU FACES Laboratory, Baton Rouge became the twenty-first M/CAP site in the country, and our lab retains a representative on the local M/CAP team.

At the FACES lab we strive diligently to assist families in bringing their loved ones home alive. We charge no fee for age progressions on missing children and adults.

13

CAPITOL

THE forensic scientist from the State Police Crime Laboratory stood waiting for me in the cool shade of the small grove of trees that covered the southeastern edge of the State Capitol grounds in Baton Rouge. I recognized George Schiro's tanned, rugged face as I rounded the corner of the old arsenal museum, actually a nineteenth-century powder magazine. I moved across the lawn dusting the dirt from the excavation unit, or pit, from my pants.

"Aha! You found me," I said.

"Yeah, your department secretary said you would be here," he replied, his youthful grin belying the seriousness of his visit. "What are you doing, looking for Huey Long's 'deduct box'?" he asked, chuckling at his own joke. Every book ever written about Louisiana's most notorious governor alleges the existence of a mysterious box that contains lots of money and perhaps documents that, if found by the

Area east of the Old Arsenal Museum in Baton Rouge, circa 1930, showing major soil removal; children's identities unknown. *Courtesy George Maher, Jr.*

right people, could have made things quite uncomfortable for Huey Long and his cronies.

"Nothing so exciting," I answered. "We're just trying to figure out if Huey left anything intact on this end of the grounds when he pushed that square block of dirt from here up to the Capitol building to surround the first floor back in the early 1930s."

"Found anything yet?"

"Not much. Just a lone burial back over there on that little knoll," I said, gesturing toward the northeast corner of the grounds.

"Oh, really?" he responded, his interest picking up.

"Don't get excited; it's not forensic. It's probably nineteenth century."

"How do you know?"

"Square nails in the coffin."

"What's he doing here?"

"Well," I began, for perhaps the twentieth time since we had found the burial a couple of days before, "you are standing on what was once hallowed ground. Before the city moved most of the burials in the 1870s, this was a huge cemetery, civilian and military." I noticed only a slight shift in George's stance. I continued, "These old grounds had hundreds, probably thousands, of historic burials dating as far back as the 1700s and 1800s, when the French, the Spanish, the English, and the Americans were here. Indians, too. You see that Indian mound at the northwest corner of the old arsenal?"

"Yeah."

"Historical accounts suggest that Indians were buried there, and American soldiers. In fact, the soldiers stuck some of their burials in aboveground tombs right on top of the mound."

"You're kidding."

"Nope. I'll go one better than that. During the Civil War, the Union troops had cannons right up there on top of the mound, in among the tombs."

"Why didn't Huey just level that mound for his dirt?" George asked.

"I don't know. Maybe he had a vision that it would bring bad luck." George smiled broadly at my attempt at humor in the blazing sun. The heat made me aware that the history session was over and that George had forensics business on his mind. "Whatcha got, George?"

"I've got some dental records for you to look at on the new case—you know, the little teenager."

I knew all right, too well. The image of her remains had been with me for most of the day, the Capitol grounds project providing only a temporary reprieve from its grisly detail.

"I'll compare these X rays to the ones I made when I get back to the lab this evening," I said, taking the small brown envelope from his hand. The envelope held the one ever-so-slight chance for a family who probably knew their daughter had been found that she might not be the person whose remains were in my laboratory.

Our business ended, George and I walked together across the grounds. We lingered for a moment at an excavation unit where a student was removing a ceramic fragment with a bit of pale purple transfer print design on it, confirming its nineteenth-century origin.

"You want to dig?" I said.

"Maybe when you schedule a project in a cooler month," he replied, beating a hasty retreat toward his car.

"When is that in Louisiana, January 14?" I hollered back and waved.

What I didn't get around to telling George that day back in 1990 was that we were also looking for ten cast-iron coffins that had been laid to rest somewhere on the Capitol grounds around 1930. Huey Long's building project had uncovered the eighteenth- and nineteenth-century burial boxes, obviously missed during the first removal in the 1870s. Old photographs, some from the Louisiana State Library and others provided by George Maher, Jr., from his private collection, showed a concrete-lined vault into which the coffins had been placed. Maher's father, George, Sr., knew Huey Long and had helped to locate a lot of the old coffins with his now famous ground radio machine, the precursor to the modern metal detector. Maher, Sr., actually discovered some of the coffins in the 1920s, before Huey's building

On the Louisiana State Capitol grounds during the 1930s, workers using the ground radio machine developed by George Maher, Sr., to locate old cast-iron coffins. *Courtesy Louisiana State Library.*

project began, when he was helping local law enforcement look for some stolen loot. He found the loot and the coffins. Later, helping Huey, he found even more coffins, but they were reburied on the grounds in an unmarked common grave.

For a moment, George's mention of Huey Long took me back to Mama's image of the Long dynasty. I wondered what she would have thought of my current archaeological project. Young and old had come out to speculate about the past. The stories the more seasoned citizens told of the 1920s and 1930s depicted a time when the Capitol's landscape was changing more rapidly than anyone could have predicted. Buildings were razed, majestic homes demolished, citizens pulled from eternal rest. For centuries men had fought and died for these grounds; now they would not give up their few remaining secrets as easily as I had hoped. The archaeological test units we had sunk here and there across the grounds gave us but brief glimpses into the past, providing us with only a small portion of its story.

As I walked toward the front of the Capitol building, through the trees I caught sight of Huey Long's statue. It stands in the garden at the edge of what some people call the South's first true skyscraper. Beneath the statue's base now rests Mama's hero, and, perhaps, even his deduct box.

I left the field early that day, putting my assistant in charge. I couldn't think about the Capitol grounds anymore. I had to compare the dental records. The family needed to know. I needed to know.

The cool air in the forensics lab felt good to my sweat-covered body. I pulled out the case file and flipped the switch for the X-ray light box to get a closer look at the small bitewings.

No doubt, it was Adrian Charlet. Damn the one who did this, I thought. Placing the X ray George had given me over one I had made

Old coffins found on the State Capitol grounds in the 1930s and reburied in this grave somewhere on the same grounds. *Courtesy Louisiana State Library.*

was like laying a transparency across a photograph. The morphology of the tooth roots, the bright white of the metal fillings, everything fit.

I was drawn once more to Adrian's final moments. Her life was way too short, ending at the tender age of nineteen. Her death was an unnecessary thing. Her body's advanced stage of decomposition left far too many mysteries. Was she surprised by her attacker? Did she have a chance to fight? Had she been harmed in other ways? Did she guess that death was near? I thought again of her remains in the other room and the trauma I would have to lay out in detail in a court of law if the perpetrator were found and tried.

As I leaned back in my chair, I could not help but think of all the women who have been abused in their lives. Reluctantly, my thoughts turned inward to my own childhood. For just a brief moment, I allowed myself to cry for Adrian, for all of those women, and for myself. Then I flipped the switch on the light box and called it a night, dreading the next day's task.

The authorities called me a few days later with the news that they had located Adrian's companion from the night that she disappeared. He had told them his side of the story admitting finally that he and Adrian had argued, then struggled. "I pushed her," he said, "and she fell, hitting her head. I was scared and hid her body." That explanation would make for an interesting trial, I reflected, given the battered state of Adrian's remains.

Get out the navy blue suit and sensible pumps, Manhein. Cover the ankle tattoo with dark stockings. Practice a slow delivery. It's showtime.

But the case never made it to trial. Adrian's companion pled guilty to manslaughter a few days before that event was to begin. His daring escape afterward from the prison where he was being held temporarily brought him only short-lived freedom. When located and confronted by sheriff's deputies, he killed himself in the front seat of his car.

We never found the cast-iron coffins.

INDIAN WOMAN

I like to use myself as an example of what our wonderful melting pot in America is like. Hill dirt may be in my blood, but ethnically, and even racially, I am a mix with ancestry among the Germans, Dutch, Scotch-Irish, Native Americans . . . maybe even others. Personally I prefer to think of myself as simply an American, though I am proud of my ethnic roots—all of them.

My great-grandmother Rena Miller was Alabama Choctaw. This information came from my great-aunt Eve Huffman when she was ninety-five—I guess it's so. In the late twentieth century it seems very popular to claim Native American roots, especially Cherokee ones. Perhaps the appeal of this tribe is due to the fact that the Cherokee— "beautiful people," as they are known—have retained an aloofness that whites grudgingly admire. Maybe it is also because the word "Cherokee" rolls off the tongue with such a lovely sound.

Working in forensic anthropology necessitates that I make statements regarding a person's racial origin. The reason is obvious: by providing a "race" designation I can help law enforcement to identify the unidentified much faster. The designation is made possible by the fact that skeletal variation does exist among the three major racial categories typically found in the United States: Caucasoid, Negroid, and Mongoloid. Caucasoid refers to people of white European descent; Negroid to those with black or African American features; and Mongoloid to Native Americans or American Indians, Asians, and Eskimos. Of course, mixed ancestry like mine complicates the job of determining a race profile, as does regional variation of features. In such cases, racial identity may still be suggested.

The variation among populations can be seen in the skull. The shape of the eye orbits, the shape of the nasal opening, alveolar prognathism (anterior protrusion of the dental arch), and projection of the cheek bones are some of the characteristics that distinguish the races. These attributes can be assessed through observations and measurements of the skull. Their differences resulted thousands of years ago from groups' long-term residence in diverse geographic areas remote from one another. There, natural selection increased the frequency, or presence, in the different gene pools of certain characteristics that were beneficial for survival. Different climates selected for both overt and subtle variations in characteristics for different populations.

Anthropology textbooks aptly point out that more variation exists within racial groups than between them. However, the forensic identification process requires a label because, in a practical sense, we humans compartmentalize other humans. One way in which we do this is by racial or ethnic designations. They help us organize our observations about our world. Noting physical variations among populations is not racism; arriving at social prejudices based on these observations, of course, is.

Many people view skin color as a criterion for race. Skin color, one of those features we immediately notice about someone, is one of the poorest of all physical characteristics by which to assess race; indeed, it is not used by anthropologists to make identifications. By 1998 there were almost 270 million people in this country—and probably very close to that many different "colors" of skin. Anthropologists debate among themselves whether biological races for humans exist, but the racial categories meaningful to them do not include the everyday descriptions of race with details like the shade of someone's skin.

Assigning a race designation and building a skeletal profile are tasks not restricted to modern forensic cases. For more than a century, anthropologists in this country have studied the physical remains of ancient Native Americans, some of which are thousands of years old. They have provided insight into the demographics and health status over time of these populations. In recent years, however, people have become particularly sensitive about the ownership or guardianship of ancient human remains, especially those of ancestral Native Americans. Indeed, many Native Americans hold present-day physical anthropologists accountable for nineteenth- and early-twentieth-century removal of their ancestors from their graves. Some of them do not like the idea of scientific study of skeletal remains in general and call for the return of all ancestral remains to extant tribes.

To demonstrate to extant Native American groups that we physical anthropologists could make a valuable contribution to the understanding of the ancient and recent past, in 1988 I traveled to South Dakota for an international conference on treatment of the dead. Only a few physical anthropologists, including Dr. Clyde Snow and myself, showed up at the meeting. I went with some trepidation owing to my brief years in the discipline at the time. However, Doctor Snow is considered by many people to be the leading forensic anthropologist in the world for his work in the recovery and identification of victims of war and other political crimes.

On the day I spoke, the auditorium was crowded to capacity with hundreds of representatives from most of the Indian nations. The climate at the meeting was clearly anti–physical anthropology. Nevertheless, I began my presentation on a case study of historic white burials to show how bioarchaeology can help to unveil mysteries about our past. Speaking quite eloquently, I naively thought, I noted how Robert Murphy, a cultural anthropologist, has suggested that anthropologists "have inherited the mythmaker's task—to explain man to mankind." Audible snorts came from the audience. The reaction only made me more determined to speak a little more firmly and a lot louder. I don't think the audience knew quite what to make of me since I had noted my Native American heritage a little earlier in my presentation.

Doctor Snow's turn at the podium was met with even more resistance when he tried to discuss some skeletal remains that had been found in what was thought to be a forensic context but in reality turned out to be a Native American burial. He didn't get far. A rather serious Native American gentleman, his arm in a cast, walked up to a microphone positioned in the center aisle of the auditorium and said to him, "Sir, if you talk about these remains at all, someone will be waiting for you when you get back to Oklahoma."

Eventually, after some debate, the symposium leader asked Dr. Snow to step down. He just smiled that lazy little smile of his and walked away. Later he told me that he knew the man in the cast; he also said he had been given permission from the tribal leaders to speak about the case. "Why, hell," he said, "I don't want to make them mad. . . . I'm married to an Indian."

Needless to say, neither one of us was invited to the sweat lodge that night.

Many years ago, when my children were small, they were feuding with my neighbor's children. Just prior to the quarrel, I had enjoyed a nice discussion with them all about heritage and pride in ancestry. When left to themselves, though, the boys got into a disagreement about something. I ignored their bickering, and the neighbor's children ran home. My boys went about their business. A little while later the neighbor called on the phone, screaming.

"Indian woman!" she shouted, and at first I gasped and paused in surprise. "Indian woman," she repeated, "can't you talk?"

At that point, I began laughing so hard at her feeble attempt to insult or enrage me—I couldn't tell exactly which—that she hung up in frustration.

Today my students and I joke about the "Indian woman" story. They tell me I simply must leave my skull to the lab some day. I tell them I might; there's no telling what my skull looks like under what I consider my funny little face!

VOODOO WOMAN

A sheriff's deputy called me one day in 1989 to ask if I could look at a skull and tell him something about it. This one wasn't found in the woods or in a grave or along the side of a road, but in a plastic bag inside a small shed behind the home of Ruby Jordan.

Who was Ruby Jordan, and what was she doing with a skull in a bag, and where was Ruby Jordan now? Ruby Jordan was dead. Allegedly, she had threatened and subsequently tried to kill her longtime boyfriend, James Robillard. Scared to death of the "voodoo woman," as he called her, Robillard simply defended himself, he told the sheriff. In the end, Ruby lay dead. Authorities confirmed Robillard's story by interviewing eyewitnesses to the event. Later they found a special altar in Ruby's house that contained voodoo paraphernalia, including potions and dolls and other trappings of a serious practitioner. The whole case could have ended there except for one thing. Ruby's children had gone to her house to remove her personal belongings in order to settle her estate: in a small outbuilding there they found the plastic bag with the human skull inside. Unnerved, they called the sheriff.

I looked at the skull and it told the story. The forehead was straight, the superior eye orbit borders were sharp. Though a fairly large skull, the muscle attachment areas were small. The skull was probably female. In addition, her eye orbits were square, almost rectangular; her nasal opening was short and broad; and in profile, her upper jaw protruded slightly. These attributes are all associated with a designation of black, or African American.

As part of my assessment, I needed to suggest an age at death. The hip bone is the best bone to use for aging up until about sixty years, but all I had was the skull.

All animals have joints, or sutures, in the skull. Humans are no exception. Those sutures, most of which are interlocking like pieces of a puzzle, are wide open when we are born to allow for growth and development. Little by little they fuse together at somewhat regular intervals in our lives. The stage of that fusion can be used generally to assess age. As we grow older still, the sutures can actually obliterate, or disappear. The sutures on the black female, case 89-14, were in the process of disappearing, and she had no teeth left in her dental arcade. She may have worn dentures in life and was probably over the age of sixty.

Attached to the sparse strands of her real hair was a short gray wig. Inside her eye sockets were the small, round plastic disks that the mortician had carefully placed there, the signature of her formal burial preparation. Inside her nasal opening were dried beetle pupae, or shells, sometimes associated with buried bodies. The color of her skull was dark brown, another sign of probable burial, perhaps as long as ten to twenty years. This older black female had once been removed. Who was she, this woman whose skull had hung at Ruby's place?

Some people said that Ruby had had a long-standing feud with her mother, who had died ten years earlier from natural causes and been buried in the family plot. Ruby's mother had owned a short gray wig. Could the skull belong to Ruby's mother? Could Ruby have opened her mother's grave to settle their disagreement? Ruby's children had only recently placed a concrete slab across their grandmother's grave. They did not wish to remove the slab, nor did they wish to know what their mother may have done. Since the indicators on the skull were those of a natural burial and since both parties were departed, if it was okay with law enforcement, they would simply let it go.

They let it go.

PROPHECY

I could not get a positive identification on 91-14. The remains had been transported to my laboratory at LSU by the sheriff's department, and my profile of the white, petite female under the age of thirty had not solved the mystery of who she was or how she had died. Her remains were held in the lab as unidentified and stayed that way for more than a year after I first worked the case.

If the standard profile I establish does not result in a positive identification, other techniques can be used to try to identify someone. One of these is clay facial reconstruction. In this technique, clay is placed over the skull to approximate what the person may have looked like in life. Facial reconstruction combines science and art. Its role is to make someone acquainted with the person in life take notice of a case, to jog a memory, to prompt the recognition that "that looks a little like so and so." Following such leads, law enforcement can then use the traditional sources of identification such as fingerprints, dental records, and even DNA mapping to provide the positive identification.

During the spring semester of 1993 I offered a course on forensic anthropology that included a segment on facial reconstruction as a strategy for addressing some of the unidentified cases still in my laboratory. I had recently been trained in facial reconstruction by Betty Pat Gatliff, one of the leading scientific sculptors in the world. Since one of my course goals was to prepare future anthropologists for work in the field, I wanted to familiarize the students with facial reconstruction techniques. One student, Christian Lejeune, drew what would turn out to be a "lucky card" when he picked up his assignment for his laboratory project. I had no idea that Christian's facial reconstruction would be identified; out of ten such reconstructions completed on old cases, only his would reach that goal. Not an artist, Christian felt a little uncomfortable in his role as "creator" of an image for the faceless young woman. I assured him of two things: that the technique would guide him and that publicity of his work might serve as the best and perhaps last chance we had to identify the woman. His facial reconstruction of 91-14 was featured in a university public relations article on our laboratory. It garnered awards for LSU's public relations department; but more important, it provided a name for 91-14.

The call from the sheriff's department was something of a surprise, coming only a week or two after the article had appeared. A father had not heard from his daughter in more than a year. He called the sheriff's department and told one of the deputies that he thought 91-14 might be his Annie. He had read the article, and though he did not think the facial reconstruction looked a lot like her, it was reminiscent enough to have checked out.

Why had it taken so long for this man to suspect that it was his daughter whom utility linemen had found, a whole year earlier, dead not more than a day or two so that fingerprints could yet be taken? The answer was simple. His last conversation with her had been when she was home in Alabama. He had reported her missing in Alabama, not in Louisiana. He had had no idea that she had gone back to Louisiana, much less back to the region where she had been raised.

It was there in her former hometown, as a little girl some eighteen years before, that she had pressed her fingers into an inked pad and recorded their prints for local law enforcement. She had been participating in a child safety program on the remote chance that some day she might be missing. A dedicated detective remembered the program from years before and searched the records in the sheriff's archives for the box of children's prints. He found the ones he needed.

17

THE BOAT

THE ocean seemed really calm that day in 1994. Sidney Johnson lazily cast his line hoping to catch just one more fish before heading home. Then off his port bow, he spotted a small boat drifting in the warm Gulf waters close to St. Mary Parish. He radioed the Coast Guard, who found a body in the boat and had it sent to the coroner's office for examination. Parish coroner Dr. Chip Metz asked for my help.

I noted that the young man, not over the age of thirty-five, was of slight build and Caucasoid, perhaps Hispanic, ancestry. The coroner's investigator explained how the homemade boat in which the victim was found contained religious materials and other items that suggested origins in Cuba. "If he was trying to get to Florida," the investigator said, "he was more than seven hundred nautical miles off course."

The young man had dental fillings, and I knew I could complete his profile easily enough. However, acquiring his medical records to

Facial reconstruction of young Cuban male *(left)*, facial reconstruction of same with mustache added *(center)*, photograph of same young Cuban male *(right)*

confirm his identification would be difficult. Doctor Metz asked that the FACES lab complete a facial reconstruction and publicize it.

Research associate Eileen Barrow glued tissue depth markers to the case's skull, markers she had cut to a specific length to represent the average soft tissue thickness of a young white male. Marker lengths vary depending on a person's age, sex, and race. Next she set brown glass eyes in their orbits and anchored them firmly into place. We always use brown eyes, not only because brown eyes are dominant over blue in the general population in this country, but more important to us, because they photograph well. Eileen then added clay, strip by strip, section by section, bringing the face back to life. Finally, she fashioned the nose, mouth, and ears by creating soft tissue with dimensions based on the size and shape of the bony substrate of the skull.

Before the likeness could be distributed on a national basis, I received word that the networking of the Cuban American Association had information on a man who had left Cuba with a friend several weeks before the boat was found. If the information was correct, the man and his friend had built the boat by hand, creating a strong seaworthy craft from bits and pieces of lumber found near their home.

They had sailed for America, never to be seen alive again.

If indeed these two Cubans were in the boat Johnson had discovered drifting toward Louisiana, only one could be accounted for. That young man probably died of dehydration, according to the pathologist. His friend was never found.

Through special assistance from the U.S. government, the young man's mother was brought to Louisiana, and she identified the boat, the clothing, and other personal items as belonging to her son. He was buried here in the United States, in the soil he so desperately hoped to reach in order to build a new life for the wife and children whom he had left behind in Cuba.

CLOUDS AND HORSES

THE approaching storm sent lightning zigzagging across the sky and thunder roaring at our heels as the other anthropologists and I headed through the woods with the horses' bones in plastic bags over our shoulders.

How had I allowed those crazy guys, Murray Marks and Doug Owsley, to talk me into this? I thought back to the phone call that had come a few days earlier. The insurance agent had been referred to our lab and told that we were a group of scientists who knew something about bone growth and development. Yeah, *human* bone growth and development. Of course, the dynamics of bone growth in different species are similar; we just don't usually look at horses, especially four at a time.

The case was straightforward, the agent said. Four thoroughbreds were dead, their bodies left in the woods. The owner wanted to claim his insurance money. The insurance carrier was cautious, concerned that the animals might have been deliberately starved to death. Could we look at the bones and suggest starvation?

No, we responded, but we could gather the remains together and ask for help from the pros at the local vet school. They were the experts on horses in general, though we occasionally dealt with a few of their "southern ends."

So we had gone off into the woods that day, the darkening sky forecasting a rising Louisiana storm. Immediate retrieval was necessary, the agent suggested, because the owner might hide the evidence. How often had we heard that in our usual forensics work!

The bones were easy to locate, and we hoped that a quick map of the site would get us out of the woods in about an hour. But one hour stretched into two, while the skies darkened considerably. I was packing the field equipment when I felt, rather than saw, a stillness that began to spread across the woods. The hair stood up on the back of my neck and I recalled vividly Aunt Penny's image on another such day more than thirty years earlier.

We were sharecropping in the bottoms that year, and the green blades of the tall corn plants rose high in the rich bottomland my father loved. Our family had been watching the sky that day, too. The chickens and the dogs were watching with us, and acting a little strange.

I remember we were not prepared for what we heard next: a loud, almost grinding noise coming from the road. It was our uncle driving his 1947 Ford, its back wheels shooting sparks with every turn because there were no tires on the two rims. He and his wife had driven the three miles to our house, terrified, because Aunt Penny had predicted a bad tornado. Their storm cellar had not been cleaned out since its collapse the spring before, and, mistakenly, they thought our house was more storm-worthy than theirs.

We had not recovered from that sight when Aunt Penny jumped from the car and demanded, "Someone bring an ax, get your Mama's Bible, then go inside."

The sky was almost dark as night that summer afternoon, but my brother and I were not about to miss Aunt Penny's show. We grabbed lemons and sugar from the kitchen table and headed out the back door, through the cornfield at the side of the house, and toward the ditch in the front yard by the giant sycamore tree, the perfect place to be in such a storm. The yellow-green sky was a sight to behold and Aunt Penny was greater still. We watched the sky and we watched Aunt Penny, her hair flying in the rising wind.

She took Mama's Bible and spent a few seconds looking for a passage. Then she laid the Bible on the ground, pointing it toward the approaching storm, as two of the world's greatest skeptics looked on with fascination. In one fell swoop, she arched the ax high over her head, drew a bead on the ground in front of her, and plunged the ax into the soil below. While she stood against the wind, we stayed in the ditch, not wanting to get caught, but also anticipating something dramatic—death or a miracle, we weren't sure which.

We don't know what happened that day. Our lemons grew soggy in our hands as we observed the cloud appear to separate down the middle and slowly move away. Aunt Penny picked up Mama's Bible and walked toward the house, a satisfied expression on her face.

A flash of lightning and the thunder's deafening roar brought me back to the horses and the 1980s. The wind picked up and rain poured down as Murray, Doug, and I ran the last half-mile through the woods toward our waiting vehicles. Lucky for us, it was not an Aunt Penny storm after all; lucky for the horse owner, fraud could not be established. The bones supplied no evidence of osteoporosis, or abnormal thinning, from long-term starvation.

19

BUGS

PERHAPS it is the smell of death that draws them toward us in the field; perhaps my O-positive blood, long thought to be attractive to things that bite and sting, makes me an especially popular target. "No-see-ums" are what we sometimes call them, and millions of them fill southern swamps. These small gnats make their way into every unprotected pore of our bodies, and they bite and bite. They swarm around in great masses as we work in the swamps and they hover over swamp burials in large gray clouds of beating wings. Their presence is one of the worst aspects about recovering a swamp burial in the summer, followed closely, of course, by that of mosquitoes.

The mosquitoes in Louisiana are like suicide pilots diving toward you with uncanny precision. Even the most effective repellents on occasion seem like aphrodisiacs for them. The female is the one who bites; most female mosquitoes require a "blood meal" before depositing their eggs. There are days when I think I have provided blood for half the newborn mosquitoes in the swamps.

Chiggers, or "red bugs," are another menace, associated with warm weather recoveries in tall grasses and wooded areas. They burrow into your skin, and you do not even know they are there until about six to eight hours later, when your whole body is itching from their bites. If you then look closely at your skin, in places you can reach, you can see tiny red dots, which reflect their presence. Usually a good insect repellent can protect you from them, a precaution you will subsequently be sure to take if ever you experience their wrath.

The gnats, mosquitoes, and chiggers torment us, but the lowly fly is one insect forensic professionals are always glad to see. Flies in Louisiana come in a variety of different species, more than 100 of them, including the common housefly, the bronze blowfly, the soldier fly, the hairy-maggot blowfly, and the "hemorrhoid fly" (so known colloquially because of its red-dotted tail area). One of the most common flies at a death scene is the secondary screwworm fly, a type of blowfly.

The reproductive life of a mature female blowfly involves laying hundreds of eggs. She arrives in minutes, sometimes even seconds, after death if the body is accessible to her and lays her eggs, or oviposits, in moist orifices—the nose, the eyes, an open wound. Then she is off, never to see her offspring.

Within eight to twelve hours after egg deposition in warm weather, the first offspring are born. The hundreds of newborn larvae, also known as maggots—and sometimes called "jumping rice"—will feed for four to five days while other flies lay new eggs, et cetera. People ask whether a body naturally has maggots on it after death. It can only have maggots on it if flies lay their eggs there; spontaneous generation of maggots does not occur.

Adult blowflies are often the first to arrive at a fresh corpse. These flies set in motion the biological clock of their offspring. The hands on this clock tell the forensic entomologist how long it has been since the person died. Because forensic entomologists study the life cycles of flies and other insects, their aid can be crucial in determination of time elapsed since death, especially if only hours or a few days are involved.

Fewer than twenty-five forensic entomologists are available for consultation in this country. My good friend Dr. Lamar Meek is one such bug man, one of the best. Though we can look out and wave hello to one another from our respective windows on the LSU campus, more often than not we exchange our greetings when we arrive independently at a scene.

If Lamar is unavailable, I can collect his bugs for him—"just a spoonful," he says—though he prefers to do his own collecting. The collection process includes careful examination of the scene and sampling of the many different fly larvae, wasps, beetles, and any other insects that are going about their business.

Even when no fly larvae appear to be present at a scene, Lamar moves out and away from the body, "tracking maggots" we call it. He probes as deeply as an inch into the soil looking for their pupae: the small, brown, bean-shaped containers from which they will emerge as mature flies after four to five more days. In preparation for this pupae stage, maggots often leave the body in mass. Though they move away from the body in all directions, primarily they head east or southeast, leaving behind a trail of brown grass, killed by their body fluids. Research conducted by Lamar and his former graduate student, Jeanine Tessmer, suggests that this southeasterly movement may be impelled by the anticipated warmth of the rising sun.

Specimens representing all of the varying generations of larvae and mature adults should be collected quickly and placed in 70 percent ethyl alcohol (ethanol) solution for best preservation. Other specimens should be collected alive and placed in a container with no alcohol. Rearing these specimens to adulthood can further confirm the different species of flies present at the scene. The types of species there may indicate a variety of things, including original location of the body. A body found in the woods, for instance, should not have housefly larvae on it since this species is most often associated with houses and barns.

In Louisiana, fire ants can also play a role in estimation of post-mortem interval. Their presence at a scene should be noted carefully because they eat fly eggs and young larvae and can skew the estimation of time since death by removing and devouring our evidence.

Like forensic anthropologists, forensic entomologists typically deal only with the dead. Nevertheless, they, too, occasionally enjoy a work-related story.

One research project that Jeanine and Lamar were conducting sought to determine whether flies lay their eggs at night—an important consideration if those eggs are used to estimate time elapsed since death. Jeanine chose plucked chickens as subjects and one night surreptitiously deposited them at various places across campus, some well lit, others much darker. Now and then during the night, she checked her subjects for fly activity. One chicken disappeared; she replaced it. Since the chickens were tied down in their small boxes and quite protected from predators, Jeanine could not figure out why the one chicken went missing.

On an errand the following week, she overheard a conversation describing how a campus employee at one location had refused to come to work the week before. He thought someone had placed a voodoo curse on him because a chicken had appeared in the courtyard one night. He removed it; it came back. Jeanine was obliged to find the frightened man and tell him that it had merely been a forensic entomology project, assuring him that her only interests in chickens were research and lunch.

In Louisiana, flies used as forensic markers do not lay their eggs at night.

20

THE LAKE

THE human skull with the three cervical vertebrae still attached to it stared back at me. Its fishy odor confirmed the officer's story that "it came up with the second load in the net."

Francis and Richard Couvillion had been out on the lake again for the weekend. As usual they would drop their net into the water and raise it frequently to see what they had landed. An occasional garfish, a frantic turtle, a rubber boot would be turned back to the lake. Lake Pontchartrain was calm that day. The clouds that were slowly moving in obstructed the view only slightly; still the Couvillions could see a few miles across the lake. Even on good days, it isn't possible to see all the way across Pontchartrain. At its maximum, it stretches for thirty miles.

Other fishermen were also on the lake that day. The Vietnamese contingent was working near the shore and their short, sharp words picked up by the wind could be heard every so often as a sort of singsong. Many Vietnamese had come to Louisiana in the early 1980s, and some had formed a large, close-knit community in New Orleans, their terraced gardens along the Mississippi River redesigning the traditional landscape.

Ten years have passed since the head came up in the net, but my experience with it seems like yesterday. As usual, I conducted my osteological analysis. The pathologist's autopsy cut neatly encircled the calva, the very top of the cranium. Putrefactive tissue still covered parts of the skull and clung tenaciously to the three vertebrae.

In general, a skull's only contact with the postcranial bones is at its base, where bony protrusions, or condyles, articulate with the first vertebra. This vertebra, called the atlas, has two smooth superior articular surfaces, or facets, that fit against the condyles. Corresponding inferior facets of the atlas articulate with the superior facets of the second vertebra, the axis, and so on down the line to include all twenty-four vertebrae. The atlas and the axis allow the head to turn from side to side and to nod, respectively. I separated the tissue from the vertebrae. The atlas and the axis were just fine. It was cervical vertebra number three that was not so fine.

On its right inferior facet, I noticed a distinctive perimortem cut. That facet would normally articulate with the superior facet on the fourth vertebra. Everything below the third vertebra was missing. The bone had been cut with a sharp instrument, probably a knife. That small cut, approximately four millimeters across, was one graphic example of the assistance that forensic anthropologists can provide to pathologists. By removing all of the tissue, we can look for small telltale signs, which can be hidden by swollen remains.

Now we knew with near certainty why the rest of the body was not with the skull. Most likely, the person had been deliberately decapitated. Sometimes in such decapitations, the third vertebra will exhibit the sort of perimortem trauma I discovered. The first two vertebrae are so close to the skull that they often remain undamaged from the sharp instrument trauma.

The skull's morphology provided other clues. The cranium was short and high vaulted. The zygomatic or cheek bones protruded slightly. The shape of the palate was rounded and the nasal opening's width was intermediate between that of black and white racial profiles. The slightly rugose, or robust, appearance of the cranium and square, masculine shape of the mandible suggested a designation of "male" for the gracile, or small, skull. Though cranial suture closure is variable, the stages of closure on the case from the lake indicated that the man probably was no older than twenty-five to thirty-five years.

Our assessment complete, we recognized the skull as that of a young Asian male. Since this case was the first one of Asian origin that had come to our laboratory, I sought confirmation of my evaluation by consulting with Dr. Richard Jantz of the University of Tennessee. He upheld my preliminary assessment after running the measurements through a software program he and other researchers had developed that assesses racial affinity.

I wish identifying the young man proved as straightforward as profiling him. His teeth were in perfect condition. So from the outset we knew that even if a putative identification were established, mechanisms other than dental records would be required to obtain a positive one. Though we completed a facial reconstruction, no putative identification was ever established. The man had been dead for only two to three weeks when his skull was found, but inquiries by law enforcement revealed no reported missing people in the local Asian community. More mystifying still, none of the rest of his body was ever found. Even now, a decade later, his identity remains unknown.

THE BAT-WING FILLING

SHE was just seventeen," the detective from north Louisiana said. What distinguished his call to my lab from the several others I received that month in 1992 was the mileage factor. "We have some bones, and we have two girls missing," he continued. "Can we bring them to you?"

Once more, as on many other occasions, I prepared myself to wait for the remains of some mother's child. My initial outrage usually settles into scientific detachment as I accept that what I do can move a family one small step toward peace of mind. Though peace of mind does not bring back a loved one, it can help the grieving process, and sometimes it is all that I can give.

The detective knocked on the lab door early the next morning. All that was left of the young teenager's life fit into one brown paper bag with the usual police identification numbers boldly printed across its front. The telltale red tape with black lettering that sealed the bag read "Evidence. Do not Tamper."

"Two young females are missing in our area, but we believe we know who this one might be," the detective noted. "She's been missing five years."

The gray, weathered, and splintered bones carefully handed to me certainly could have been exposed on the earth's surface for that length of time. These few bones had been widely scattered across a wooded area. The detectives found them only after searching relentlessly for days.

Sitting in the county jail, James Bryson, in a talkative mood, had bragged to Johnny Smith about a young girl in a burger restaurant uniform that he had "gotten rid of" years before. Johnny Smith made a deal with authorities.

Law enforcement took over after that, combing the woods for the remains of Amy Pearson. They found an arm bone, a leg bone, a portion of a skull, and finally, the lower jaw. In that jaw only one tooth had a filling, but it was all Dr. Vincent Lagatutta, forensic odontologist, needed to confirm my preliminary identification. Amy Pearson had been found. The antemortem records made by Amy's dentist showed one molar with a filling that resembled a bat with wings. Our postmortem radiograph matched them perfectly. The shapes were identical.

The last time her mother saw Amy Pearson was the afternoon when she bounced out the door, her short brown hair almost completely hidden beneath the hat she wore for her job at the hamburger place downtown.

She never made it home that evening. For five years, her family looked for her, knowing she must be dead, hoping, at least, that her body might be found.

Though her physical remains could not tell us exactly what happened to her, the upcoming trial of the accused would at least provide Amy Pearson with her day in court. James Bryson must have worried just a little about that day. Less than an hour before Lagatutta and I were to board our plane for the trip to the trial, Bryson admitted his guilt in exchange for life without parole.

BAYOU BLEU

HOW long can a six-week-old baby last if thrown into a bayou?" the assistant district attorney calmly asked me on the phone one afternoon. I felt the sandwich I had just wolfed down for lunch rising in my throat.

When the two bayou detectives entered the forensics lab, their sharp after-shave introduced a welcome freshness to the stale air. "The case is fairly simple," the clean-shaven, serious officer said, his piercing eyes looking directly into mine.

I hoped he was right.

"The informant told us where to look, and we looked just where he said, and we found it, the body . . . the skeleton, that is."

"Well, how can I help you?" I responded.

"Tell us what happened to her," Piercing Eyes said, "and tell us, if you can, where the baby might be."

With one look at the adult woman's skeleton, I knew I could respond with information to the first request. The second one was an entirely different matter.

"Well," I began again, hating to be put on the spot, but understanding their hurry—everyone wants an instant answer—"it looks like a bullet wound to the back of the head." That part was obvious. What was not so obvious was where the bullet went after it entered the head. I turned the skull over in my hands, noting that the fragile bones of the right eye orbit were broken, some missing altogether. The bullet may have taken the easy way out—straight through and through. Quite often, as a bullet moves through the skull, it will leave a track of small metal fragments, called "bullet wipe," from its breakup, defining its route. A quick X ray could provide evidence that would confirm or deny my suspicion.

I took anterior, posterior, and lateral shots of the skull. The developed X rays showed the course the bullet had taken with bright white spots moving across the vault and toward the eye—straight through and through.

My earlier conversation with the assistant DA had not left me, nor had I forgotten the detectives' second request of me. "What about a baby?" I asked.

The voice of Piercing Eyes grew a little strained. "The victim allegedly had her baby with her; the baby has not been found. Bayou Bleu is very close to where she was found."

"What?" I said, feeling a terrible sadness rise up within me. "Do you think the baby went into the bayou?"

He shrugged his shoulders and looked away.

"How long has it been since this happened?" I whispered.

"Almost a year," he said. He gazed steadily at me and asked again, "Where do you think the baby might be?"

"In God's hands," I said.

The defendant looked so innocent at the trial, his youthful face arguing against his capacity to commit these unspeakable horrors: murder of the mother of his child, murder of the child. The prosecution argued that he had killed the mother in order not to pay child support and that he had then thrown the baby into the bayou. An eyewitness to the crime testified as much for the State, saying he had not been able to sleep well since the incident had occurred.

Conviction was fast, final. But the life of this former police officer was spared, and instead he was sent to prison for life without parole. This person, who had sworn an oath to protect his fellow man, was in the end saved by his eight-year-old son's plea, "Please don't kill my daddy."

We never found the baby.

23

WHO KILLED HUEY LONG?

THE crowd that gathered at the cemetery on North Street in Baton Rouge that day back in 1991 was not so different from the one that had scrambled into the State Capitol chambers some fifty-six years earlier. They shared a common goal: they wanted a glimpse of the alleged assassin of Huey Long, Dr. Carl Austin Weiss. Of course, Dr. Weiss's family, as well as forensic scientists—including those from George Washington University, the Smithsonian Institution, and my laboratory at LSU—were also there to look at the legendary doctor.

Though no longer governor of Louisiana at the time of his death, Huey Long still ruled the state with an iron hand. The often-told story goes that on September 8, 1935, Dr. Weiss, a young Baton Rouge physician, walked into the State Capitol and shot Senator Long. In turn, Long's bodyguards shot Weiss. Weiss died instantly; Long died a couple of days later. Weiss, a Catholic, was given a proper Christian burial in a Clarke vault in the cemetery on North Street.

The controversy surrounding the death of Huey Long has plagued historians for years. Several months prior to the exhumation, James Starrs, a professor at George Washington University, and Dr. Douglas Ubelaker, curator of physical anthropology at the Smithsonian Institution, had spoken with the Weiss family about the possibility of exhuming Weiss. Clarke advertised its vault as "guaranteed for life." If the vault was still sealed, then some soft tissue might be preserved. If so, the body might contain clues as to why Weiss acted the way he allegedly did more than fifty years ago, clues that modern technology could help decipher. The family agreed to the exhumation.

Crowds pushed at the ropes, trying to get a closer view as the metal vault was raised from its shallow grave. The vault's weight necessitated that the coffin be removed from it before being transported to the Lafayette Crime Laboratory, the site chosen for analysis. Starrs would not allow the body to be taken to my laboratory at LSU.

In keeping with Clarke's guarantee, the vault was still sealed, but the wooden coffin inside had fallen apart. The body was no longer intact. Hastily, in situ X rays were taken to document any metal fragments, which could shift in transit to Lafayette. Though very little tissue was still intact, the bones would reveal part of Weiss's story.

We were especially interested in the hands. One account associated with that long-ago evening suggested that rather than shooting at Long, Weiss had simply struck out at him with his fist. If that were true, his metacarpals, the first row of tubular bones in his hand, might have perimortem fractures.

At the laboratory in Lafayette, I began to clean the bones. As I gently brushed away debris from Weiss's right and left hands, I looked for fracture evidence. Though a few small fracture lines were noted, Ubelaker later confirmed that they were simply from postmortem drying. Because thorough analysis of the remains would take weeks, Ubelaker decided it would best be completed in his laboratory at the Smithsonian. Ultimately, he and Starrs published a report on this historic case.

Ubelaker found that Weiss's skeleton exhibited more than twenty gun-shots wounds, with at least 50 percent or more of the bullets entering the body from the back. In his archival investigation, Starrs located a gun that Weiss had purchased in France several years before the Capitol incident. In 1997 the gun was donated to the State of Louisiana by the Weiss family and is now on display at the Old State Capitol Museum in Baton Rouge.

The truth about what happened back in 1935 remains somewhat elusive. The inconclusiveness of the recounted "facts" bothers me. I've never been convinced that Weiss killed Huey Long. Some suggest that my view of events is clouded by the fact that I am female. I laugh at this condescension. History notes that Weiss was a happy man. He was a promising young doctor with a new baby son. It was reported that he had been on a family outing that afternoon prior to the Capitol incident. I weigh his future with his family and his career that held such hope and promise against the certain death that he must have known would await him in the Capitol if he shot Long. His alleged assassination of the senator doesn't make sense.

But why did he go to the Capitol that day? Some say it was to kill Huey Long. Others say he simply wanted to talk there with Long about Long's treatment of Weiss's father-in-law. Still others hint of a conspiracy involving Weiss to eliminate the senator, who was well into his campaign for presidency of the United States.

Some who doubt Weiss's guilt suggest that Long was killed accidentally by an overzealous group of new bodyguards, a stray bullet from a trigger-happy, inexperienced enforcer ending his life at forty-two. Even more intriguing, according to Louisiana State Police Crime Laboratory ballistics expert Patrick Lane, is the fact that settlement of an insurance policy on Long notes "accidental death."

The lone, spent bullet that was stored with Weiss's gun—the gun that moved mysteriously from law enforcement to private possession, and finally back to the Weiss family—was not fired by that gun.

Patrick Lane confirmed this fact. Was it a bullet that was removed from Long's body? Does it have any association whatsoever with this case? No one seems to know.

Indeed, we may never know what really happened on the day Huey Long died, but what if the real evidence were buried with him, not with Carl Weiss? Would exhumation of Long provide any assistance in solving this mystery? Could the bullet trajectory for the death-dealing wound or wounds to Long's body suggest from which direction the shot, or shots, was fired? Could scanning electron microscopy or other technological advances reveal the signature of a yet-undiscovered metal object, confirming or denying Weiss's guilt?

Famous persons no longer rest easy in their graves. Exhumations or requests for exhumation of such personalities as Zachary Taylor, Butch Cassidy and the Sundance Kid, Meriwether Lewis (of Lewis and Clark), and Lizzie Borden's family, among others, have made national headlines. I recognize that such cases have a certain appeal. However, the sensationalism of media attention that often surrounds these types of cases makes me uncomfortable. I worry that the lines between scientific knowledge and private gain have become blurred.

Does the world have the right to know the answers to the questions surrounding Huey Pierce Long's death? Though Patrick Lane and others are not convinced that Weiss didn't kill Long, I now believe some restraint must be exercised to slow the current trend of digging up famous persons to "get to the truth." In the case of her hero—Louisiana governor and senator, and would-be-president—Mama certainly would agree.

24

A WITCH'S TALE

HISTORIC cemeteries dot the landscape across this country, and I am drawn to them, from the smallest, overgrown plot along the side of the road to the largest, manicured city of the dead. Cemeteries or tales of cemeteries were an integral part of my childhood. Grave cleaning and the subsequent "dinner on the grounds" were included in our pilgrimages to Old State Line Cemetery, where my great-aunts and uncles, Great-grandma Wallis, and other family members are buried. As children, we anxiously made the two-hour ride in the back seat of Aunt Pearl's old green and white Buick. She drove slowly down the dusty dirt roads where wilting palmettos pushed their fingerlike leaves from the earth toward the sky as we traveled deeper and deeper into the backwoods. The periodic trips to Old State Line reestablished our departed family's presence in our lives and reassured the living that they, too, might receive such attention in the future.

We spent the long day cleaning and weeding around the shallow soil depressions, rearranging dirt into mounds that served as reminders of people's lives. As Mama moved her hoe deftly back and forth across the graves, she told stories from her childhood to all those who gathered to listen. She talked about an eerie light in the cornfield at night, its source unknown. She described the hanging tree in the bend not far from her house and recalled how her family never drove a wagon that way at dusk because the horse would always bolt as it neared the dying tree. She spoke softly of the moving light seen late at night on an isolated railroad track, a brakeman from the distant past. She comforted ailing family members, assuring cousin Attie and others that she would tend to their plots if they left this world before she did.

I have not been to Old State Line since I was a child. Instead, I mind the graves of others.

In a small cemetery on the outskirts of Zachary, Louisiana, rests the above-ground burial vault of a young woman named Alice Penny Taylor. Alice died in 1859. Legend has celebrated her relation by marriage to the alleged nephew of Zachary Taylor, Mexican War hero and last U.S. president from the Deep South until Jimmy Carter was inaugurated over a century later. But her local claim to fame revolves around her reputation as the witch of Zachary.

In Louisiana, where one is more apt to hear of a voodoo priestess "working a little gris-gris," the accusation of witchery is a little uncommon. How did it come to be leveled at Alice? What were the actual circumstances surrounding her life? Hers was a story I wanted to know more about.

It all began in the summer of 1990. Wayne Rogillo, from the cemetery maintenance board in Zachary, called looking for "the Bone Lady" and reached my lab. Hearing of our scientific interest in human skeletal remains, he asked if I would like to examine the bones of a young woman whose grave had been disturbed for the third, and what he hoped would be the final, time. Of course I agreed. By piecing together what Rogillo, one of the guardians of the cemetery, told me, by

Alice Penny Taylor's original crypt showing iron railings and broken marble cover

interviewing local citizens, and by examining the physical and historical evidence, I learned a lot about Alice and a little about how the modern myth of her witchcraft has survived.

The small cemetery where Alice rested contained traditional below-ground burials except for one above-ground burial vault near the highway—hers. Contrary to popular belief, above-ground burial vaults in Louisiana began not from necessity due to flooding, but from a cultural tradition brought here by Europeans hundreds of years ago. However, they are also practical in low-lying areas prone to flooding.

Alice's reputation as a witch goes back at least two generations— to the children of the 1950s and 1960s. Alice was only nineteen years old when she died. Who knows who was the first to whisper that "a witch is buried there"? Somehow the idea began to circulate—and it stuck. The story goes that Alice roamed the cemetery at night, mournfully calling for her loved ones. Her tomb became a place where teenagers went in groups, especially on Halloween, but not alone. Quite often, if one or more of the teenagers had too much to drink, that person—typically a male—might be left in the cemetery, eventually awakening there alone and swearing never again to touch "the evil brew."

Motivation for the first violation of Alice's crypt is unknown. Perhaps it was curiosity as to what was really buried in the vault; or perhaps the violation was a simple act of robbery or vandalism. What is known is that a member of the cemetery board discovered Alice's remains lying on the ground one morning. Someone had managed to shove the marble cover aside and take her from her coffin. Caretakers placed her back inside her crypt and tried to stabilize the cover. They placed iron bars around the perimeter of the vault to hold the marble in place. The iron bars served to "hold her in," according to the local teenagers, and her reputation increased in intensity to the point where she was viewed as a murderess who roamed Zachary at night.

Again she was removed from her vault, and again. The third and most recent time, the marble cover was damaged, broken in several pieces, and that prompted the cemetery board to call me.

When my students and I arrived at the cemetery, we could tell that it would take the strength of several men to finish removing the heavy marble from Alice's tomb, confirmation that the most recent vandal had not acted alone. We gingerly removed the cover and peered into the vault. Inside was a lightweight coffin, possibly made of tin and zinc. It had the traditional glass viewing window at the head region, though the glass had fallen from place and lay on the floor of the crypt. Unfortunately for Alice, the base of her coffin had deteriorated and was separated from the sidewalls and top.

When we had lifted out the largest piece of coffin, Alice still rested on the floor of the coffin inside the crypt. We could tell that though she was in basic anatomical position, many of her remains had been shuffled about. We transported her and her coffin to my laboratory at

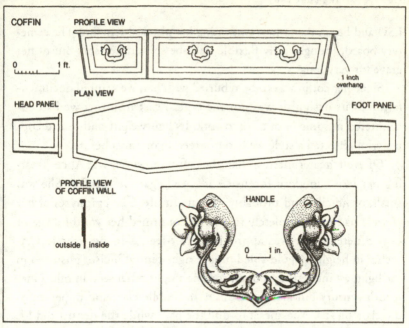

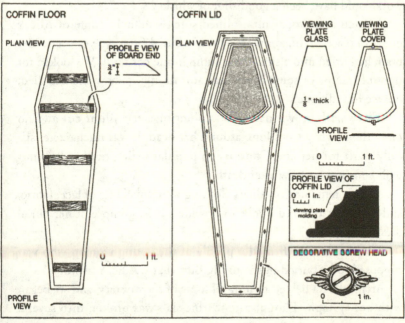

Scale drawings of Alice Penny Taylor's coffin

LSU and began the task of examining her physical remains. The cemetery board, though fairly flexible, felt she should not stay out of her grave for very long.

Since her coffin was to be reburied with her, we wanted documentation of its design. It was not the typical cast-iron sort we had encountered in some of our other work. Its lightweight nature and copper trim reflected a style we had not seen in our area before.

Of even greater interest than the coffin, however, was Alice. Treating her like a modern forensic case, we began her profile. She was small, or gracile, and probably delicate in life. The epiphyses of her clavicle had not completely fused and confirmed her youthful age of only nineteen. She was approximately 5-feet, 2-inches to 5-feet, 3-inches in height. A gold-filled, upper right central incisor glistened in the light, an interesting though common sight often seen in mid-nineteenth-century burials of persons with middle-class and upper–middle-class means. Anesthesia to dull the pain while the dentist did his work could have been a good shot of whiskey.

A small amount of mummified soft tissue held some of Alice's bones in place, an uncommon sight in a burial from 150 years ago. Her brain had dried into a small hard lump inside her skull. We looked for signs of trauma or some other indicator to suggest how she had died, but we found none.

Alice's dark brown hair was another mystery. Blunt cut and no more than eight inches long around her head, it was uncharacteristically short for her era. Contrary to popular belief, neither hair nor nails continue to grow after death.

All that remained of Alice's clothing were small bits of lace, fabric, and a few buttons and hooks to provide a brief glimpse of her burial dress.

The remains confirmed a profile of the young woman who was supposed to be buried in the tomb. But what was her real story?

Archival data helped to unravel some of the mystery, and we began with her epitaph. Though the marble slab was broken into several pieces, the verse etched into its surface belied the recent claim of witchery. Most likely composed by the loving hand of a bereaved husband, the verse read:

> Sacred to the memory of Alice A. Penny, consort of Issac Simpson Taylor, born January 28, 1840. Died December 29, 1859. Alice you are not forgot. The stone that hides your lovely form from our view, cannot hide your sweet image from our hearts. Tongue cannot tell how much we loved you. We love thy memory still. We know you are not lost but gone before. You cannot return to us, but we shall go to you.

"Consort" is a term often used in the past to refer to a man's wife. The claim that Alice's husband, Issac Simpson Taylor, was the nephew of Zachary Taylor has not been confirmed. His family, like that of Zachary Taylor, was not from Louisiana. Like Zachary, he, too, resided along the Mississippi River in the 1800s. Zachary's home was the old Spanish commandant's house that still stood on the State Capitol grounds in Baton Rouge in the 1840s and was a favorite tourist attraction for the paddle-wheelers that plied the river at that time. The story goes that whenever the captain of a boat spotted Zachary Taylor with his eyeglass, he blew his horn and everyone rushed to the side of the boat to see the famous Mexican War hero, soon to be president of the United States, as he strolled in his front yard near the river's edge.

Though there are both "Issacs" and "Alices" in Zachary Taylor's genealogy, the families seem to have come from different areas of the country and settled regions separate from one another. Zachary's relatives were from Virginia, and he came to Baton Rouge as a young military officer who was stationed at the U.S. arsenal on the current State Capitol grounds in downtown Baton Rouge. For their part, Issac's family originated in Pennsylvania and moved from there to Kentucky, to Mississippi, and finally to Louisiana around the turn of the nineteenth century.

Coincidentally, Issac's home was just upriver from the Capitol

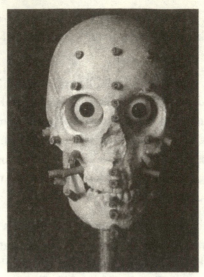

Plaster cast of Alice Penny Taylor's skull
with tissue depth markers attached

grounds and was located on a point not too far from where Southern University now stands. In the historic record, his holdings, though less than three hundred acres—including the lowland area on Bayou Baton Rouge called Devil's Swamp—were referred to as a plantation called Ashland. Ashland may have been in sight of Zachary's house just downriver. I can imagine someone saying, "There's Zachary Taylor's house, and right upriver there is Issac Taylor's place, Ashland. . . . Maybe Issac is Zachary's nephew!"

It was to Ashland that Issac took his bride, Alice, but it was to the Plains where he carried her to be buried shortly thereafter. Records suggest they were married for only a year. In the Plains, Issac placed his wife among her ancestors, the Pennies. Family history notes that she may have died either carrying or giving birth to a child.

And what of her short, cropped hair? Oral tradition states that it was not uncommon to cut a woman's hair if she were very ill, especially if she had the fever. Did Old Yellow Jack, the yellow fever, strike her as it did many thousands during the mid-1800s in Louisiana? We will never know: invasive bone samples to test for antibodies were not permitted.

Though a history of the Plains confirms Alice's family ties, someone other than her family minds her grave. Occasionally, through the years, an unknown person places flowers on her crypt. Perhaps they represent the conscience of a teenager grown to manhood.

I wondered how a lifelike image of Alice would look, this young woman, fallen from grace through no fault of her own. Such an image might help to make the dark reputation go away. No known photograph of Alice exists, so from her skull we made a mold; from the mold we cast a plaster likeness; to the plaster we added the forensic markers we use today for modern forensic cases. The facial reconstruction of Alice completed by art student Marcus McAllister is the

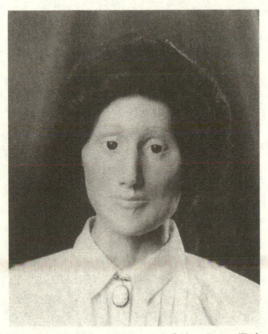

Completed facial reconstruction of Alice Penny Taylor

basis for how we now perceive her. Pinned at Alice's neck is a locket, a personal touch I added near the project's end. Inside the locket are two baby pictures, one of each of my two sons, a fact they are only learning now.

Alice's bones are back in her coffin, back in her crypt, and covered with cement. For those who believe that Issac, her husband, was nephew to a famous man, I fear it is not so. Issac died in 1866 and his beloved Ashland and other holdings were sold that year to satisfy—what else?—taxes.

25

DURALDE'S RETURN

THE cemetery caretaker stumbled as he walked across the grass that day in early 1991. Where had the hole come from that caught his boot and almost made him fall? After a peek into the opening and a fast withdrawal, he went scurrying to the church office. A cast-iron coffin rested in a shallow subterranean vault; the recent rains had exposed and dislodged the brick cover, which had gone unnoticed on the manicured lawn for more than one hundred years.

St. Joseph's Cemetery board asked for my help in sorting out the identity of the person in the coffin. When my assistants and I removed the topsoil covering the subterranean vault, we saw the shallow brick crypt had been constructed by a true craftsman, its arched roof suggesting a slightly rounded appearance. Though below-ground, brick-lined vaults are sometimes found in historic cemeteries, they are not as common as the above-ground vaults often associated with Louisiana's majestic cities of the dead.

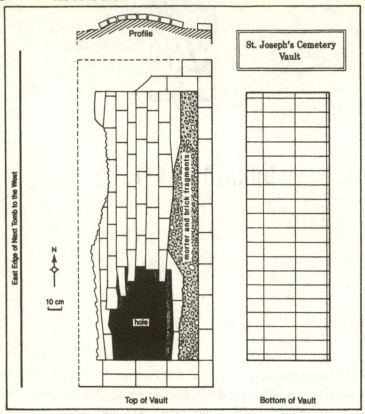

Scale drawings of below-ground vault found in St.
Joseph Cemetery, Baton Rouge

Once the crypt was completely exposed, we noted that water had managed to make its way inside the coffin. Four men struggled to lift it from its resting place. Transport to my laboratory at LSU was necessary in order to properly identify the origin of the coffin and the person inside.

At the laboratory we documented the rare old coffin, noting that the volume of water it contained, when translated into weight, exceeded five hundred pounds. Though cast-iron coffins were popular in Louisiana in the 1700s and 1800s, their cost, averaging twenty to thirty dollars, often relegated their use to the upper–middle-class and wealthy citizenry. The coffin now resting in my lab might have been a little more expensive.

It was oval shaped rather than the typical toe-pincher we often see. "Toe-pincher" is the label used to describe those coffins, both wooden and metal, that widen out at the shoulders and narrow considerably toward the feet. Our coffin had no identifying mark from a prominent coffin maker like Fisk of the kind often stamped into the metal at the foot or at the head. It did, however, offer an amazing view of the body. Unlike the coffins with the more common single-glass viewing win-

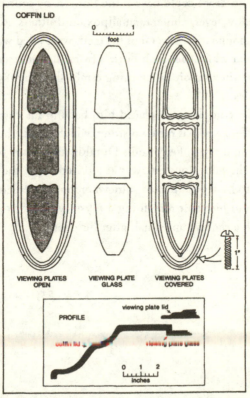

Scale drawings of coffin found in vault at St. Joseph Cemetery

dow, this one from St. Joseph's possessed three. Also, it boasted six intricately shaped handles for lifting.

When the metal plates covering the glass windows were removed, we saw that one of the pieces of glass had been dislodged years before. It rested inside the coffin, and the opening provided the perfect path for water to enter during heavy rains.

The coffin contained the remains of a young, white male. Since the seal of pitch had been broken for a considerable period of time, no soft tissue was preserved, only bone. Epiphyses on some of his long bones and other bones were unfused. He most likely died between the ages of fifteen and eighteen. No perimortem trauma was noted on his skeleton, but his death could have come from many sources as the epidemics of yellow fever, cholera, smallpox, and others crossed all socioeconomic boundaries. Several of his teeth were filled with gold, entirely consistent with other such burials from the nineteenth century. The machine stitching on his clothing established the 1850s as a base time for his death.

Our profile complete, we placed him back in his coffin and back in his crypt. Today he has his own stone, which marks the location of his below-ground crypt. Felix Louis Duralde died at the tender age of seventeen in the mid-1800s. He was accounted for in the records and known only to have been buried somewhere in the cemetery, the positive location of his vault remaining a mystery until his postmortem trip to my lab a century and a half after his death.

26

CIVIL WAR ON THE BLUFF

ON a Pleistocene bluff that rises high above the abandoned flood-plain of the Mississippi River north of Baton Rouge lies a small ceme-tery with direct ties to the American Civil War. The Port Hudson Sol-diers' Cemetery lies in an area that was part of the scene of a major battle of that war. From May 23, 1863, until July 9, 1863, one of the longest continuous battles of any war involving American troops took place at Port Hudson. Unfortunately, the American troops were bat-tling one another.

For centuries, the "white bluffs" at Port Hudson have intrigued ex-plorers, politicians, and scientists. Sieur d'Iberville, the great Canadian explorer, described their beauty and intrigue; Great Britain drew up formal plans to place a city there; Sir Charles Lyell, the famous English geologist, visited Port Hudson on his last excursion to the Americas in the 1840s.

Confederate grave marker on bluff at Port Hudson

In a region close to the bluff's edge lie several rows of small, flat, marble grave markers, approximately twenty inches long and twelve inches high. Each stone is engraved UNKNOWN CONFEDERATE SOLDIER and rests at the head of a symmetrical, shallow soil depression. In the 1960s, during the centennial memorial of the Civil War, Louisiana governor Jimmy Davis commissioned the placement of these marble markers over each of the depressions at Port Hudson. It had been suggested that the depressions represented the long lost graves of Confederate soldiers who had died during the battle there in 1863.

Over the years, vandalism and erosion had impacted the site. Two decades after the markers were laid, LSU anthropologists were asked to authenticate whether there actually were any burials at the site, and, if so, to determine whether they were soldiers. That field project began in 1987 under the direction of Doug Owsley and continued for six years thereafter under my direction. My co–principal investigator during all of those years was Ann Whitmer, a fine historic and prehistoric archaeologist.

Historically, the siege at Port Hudson is considered by some to have been one of the major turning points of the war. When the Confederates surrendered on July 9 after the fall of Vicksburg two days before, the Union army gained control of the Mississippi River and, by extension, the Red, the Black, and the Ouachita Rivers, cutting off all major water supply routes for the Confederates to the west and north.

Records suggest that approximately 1,500 Union soldiers and 200 Confederate soldiers died in battle or from associated illnesses related to the siege at Port Hudson. The casualties, though, were much greater, as more than 35,000 Union troops encircled and eventually closed in on the 6,000 or so Confederates who were surrounded on all sides.

The town of Port Hudson was destroyed. What began as a bawdy, bustling port in the early 1800s never regained its prewar stature, and a cow pasture now sits where Main Street thrived.

In 1867 the National Cemetery at Port Hudson was opened. That year marked the beginning of a massive effort either to relocate all known Union soldiers to such national cemeteries or to transport them home. In the past, it was thought that no Confederate soldiers were buried at the National Cemetery at Port Hudson. However, cemetery records indicate that at least a few may be. They may not be the only unofficial residents of the cemetery. Those folks hired to find the Union soldiers were paid "by the burial" and are said to have profited from a few not-so-human skeletal remains.

While it is likely that only a few Confederate soldiers may have ended up at the National Cemetery, the location of the majority of the two hundred or more who died at Port Hudson was not known. Some people believed that they were buried on the western edge of the old town cemetery, high on the bluff, where Governor Davis placed the stones in the 1960s. Bioarchaeology tells a somewhat different story.

Our archaeological team tested those depressions in 1987, and, yes, they were graves. However, soil stains outlining the shapes of deteriorated coffins suggested graves of adults and children. Additionally,

Testing of depressions associated with Confederate grave markers

burial artifacts were civilian in nature: plain porcelain buttons, a broken watch, and coffin hardware postdating the war. Nothing of a military nature was found.

Then we moved east of the known cemetery boundaries, and we found them—the coffin stains just below the surface once again delineating the graves. Although the bones had almost totally disintegrated, the artifacts told the story. We tested fifteen graves the first season and what we found surprised even us: buttons, buttons, and more buttons—in all the graves—and all military in origin. There was the block "I" of the Confederate Infantry, the script "I" of the Confederacy, pewter buttons, porcelain buttons . . . and the biggest surprise of all, Union Eagle buttons—U.S. military issue. The buttons were stark evidence supporting our conclusion that it was neither a Confederate burial ground nor a Union burial ground, but a soldiers' burial ground—perhaps with friend and foe buried together.

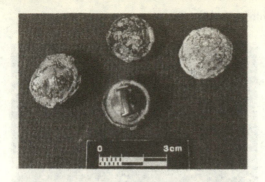

Military buttons found in soldiers' graves at Port
Hudson: Block "I" of Confederate infantry; script
"I" of the Confederacy; and Union eagle buttons.
Front center block "I" and script "I" Confederate
buttons are from a private collection.

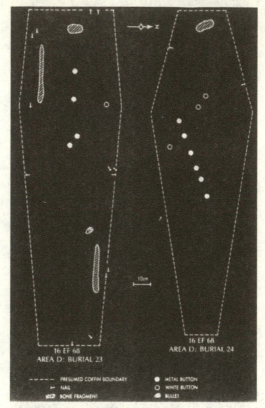

Scale drawings of soldiers' burials found at Port
Hudson. Solid white circles represent metal military buttons found in situ in the graves.

Judging by the buttons, we believe that both Union and Confederate soldiers could be buried in the little cemetery on the bluff at Port
Hudson. They may be burials that took place during the early part of
the battle. Later in the battle, surrounded on all sides, the Confederates could not have spent time or energy constructing coffins from
wood and nails they did not have. Our findings did not really surprise
us, for we had read accounts of young men who became friends across

the darkened recesses of the bluffs and the gullies that dominate the landscape of the region. They may have ended up together in the hospital of the opposing side and may have been buried together on the bluff.

From 1987 until 1991 we tested depressions throughout the hills and gullies at Port Hudson. Some depressions represented the graves of soldiers, others private citizens who lived in the region prior to the battle. Bioarchaeology helped to put to rest the questions surrounding the origin of the graves in the woods.

In 1990 a special dedication ceremony was held at the Louisiana State Commemorative Area at Port Hudson to pay tribute to all soldiers who died there. A group of Civil War reenactors and a modern military honor guard escorted a gun carrier, which bore a wooden coffin as it slowly moved across the grounds. It contained the sparse remains of victims of both armies and, following the ceremony, was carefully lowered to its final resting place beneath the single obelisk that honors them all.

Gun carrier escorted by Civil War reenactors and modern military honor guard transporting coffin to Port Hudson grave site

Flag-draped coffin containing remains of soldiers, from both the Confederate and Union armies, who died during the Battle at Port Hudson

Obelisk honoring all soldiers who died
at Port Hudson in 1863

27

FOR THOSE WHO WAIT

WHAT famous cases are out there that you would like to solve?"
is a question people often ask me. My answer sometimes surprises
them. Media attention immediately focuses on any new or rehashed
evidence regarding high-profile deaths, such as the assassination of
John Fitzgerald Kennedy, the tragic demise of Marilyn Monroe, the
disappearance of Jimmy Hoffa, or the whereabouts of Adolf Hitler's
remains. Plenty of sleuths track these stories. Though I have my own
theories about these cases and have read various accounts over the
years by those who claim to offer "new evidence," I am not strongly
drawn to famous personalities. I prefer, instead, to use my energies toward identifying my own cases who remain without names. My "wish
list" includes real names for the John and Jane Does who wait in my
lab. These are some of their stories.

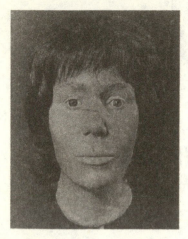

West Baton Rouge Parish case

Ascension Parish case

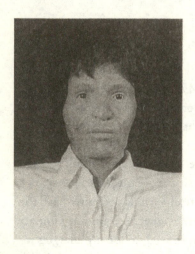

Calcasieu Parish case

Beauregard Parish case

In early 1985 a small white female, somewhere between the ages of twenty-four and thirty-two, was found on the river bank in West Baton Rouge Parish near Port Allen, Louisiana. She had been dead between three and six months. She was approximately 5-feet, 3-inches to 5-feet, 5-inches tall. She had good dental work and could be identified with dental records. Who is she?

A young white male between twenty-five and thirty-five years of age was found on June 13, 1991, in McElroy's Swamp in Ascension Parish, near Sorrento, Louisiana. He had been dead between one and two weeks when discovered. He had shoulder-length brown hair, with a few streaks of gray, pulled back in a ponytail secured with a rubber band. He had excellent dental work, including a removable bridge. He also had a diagonal scar across his right abdomen. Finally, he was wearing a pierced earring that was made from a human tooth set in gold. Who is he?

In December 1991 a young white female, possibly of Mexican or Native American heritage, was found in Calcasieu Parish near Vinton, Louisiana, just south of Interstate 10. She had been dead for just a few days when authorities found her body. She was only twenty-three to thirty years of age. She had medium-length brown hair, stood around 5-feet, 4-inches tall, and weighed between 100 and 115 pounds. A small ring with a bird image and turquoise, as well as other jewelry, was found near her. She has dental fillings that could help to identify her, and we believe there is a chance that she may be from Texas or other points farther west. She remains unidentified.

In 1993 a black male between thirty and forty years old was found in a wooded area in Beauregard Parish in southwestern Louisiana. He had been dead for several months when found. His teeth were in perfect condition; no cavities or fillings were present in his mouth. He was between 5-feet, 7-inches and 5-feet, 9-inches tall. Who is he?

St. John the Baptist Parish case   Madison Parish case

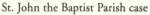

On April 2, 1994, a forty-eight- to fifty-eight-year-old white male was found in a lightly wooded area in St. John the Baptist Parish. He had been dead from two to four weeks. He had bird tattoos across his chest, and "B 4 Lynn" tattooed on his left arm; another tattoo with "Mother" and wings adorned his left forearm. He had a surgical pin in his knee and very few teeth in his mouth. He remains unidentified.

In December 1994 a young white female between the ages of eighteen and twenty-five was found in Madison Parish near Tallulah, Louisiana, just off Interstate 20. She had been dead for a minimum of two months and perhaps as long as a year. She was approximately 5-feet, 4-inches to 5-feet, 6-inches tall and of medium build. She was wearing a "Team NFL" T-shirt. She has dental fillings and very distinctive front teeth. Who is she?

Still others wait in our laboratory: the fifteen- to eighteen-year-old white female with long, light brown hair found in a wooded area in central Louisiana in 1980; the eighteen- to twenty-three-year-old white male found floating in the Mississippi River near Darrow, Louisiana, in 1982; the white middle-aged male found in 1985 who had almost all of his teeth crowned with porcelain . . . and on and on. Who were they in life?

In 1998 the FACES lab at LSU, in conjunction with the LSU Dental School, began a new database on all the unidentified people found in Louisiana. Using dental-identification software especially developed for this type of use—called "WIN-ID"—we enter all unidentified forensic cases into the database. Then we add in profiles and available dental records on the missing people from our state as well as others. The database greatly facilitates our ability to find matches where they exist.

Over the years, cases come and go through the FACES Laboratory, both forensic and archaeological in nature, hundreds and hundreds of them, each with its own special story. Concerning those missing persons, both living and dead, whom we are able to reunite with their families, we are grateful for our role in providing some peace of mind. For those whose stories do not yet have an ending, we persevere.

FOR THE BEST IN PAPERBACKS, LOOK FOR THE

In every corner of the world, on every subject under the sun, Penguin represents quality and variety—the very best in publishing today.

For complete information about books available from Penguin—including Penguin Classics, Penguin Compass, and Puffins—and how to order them, write to us at the appropriate address below. Please note that for copyright reasons the selection of books varies from country to country.

In the United States: Please write to *Penguin Group (USA), P.O. Box 12289 Dept. B, Newark, New Jersey 07101-5289* or call 1-800-788-6262.

In the United Kingdom: Please write to *Dept. EP, Penguin Books Ltd, Bath Road, Harmondsworth, West Drayton, Middlesex UB7 0DA.*

In Canada: Please write to *Penguin Books Canada Ltd, 90 Eglinton Avenue East, Suite 700, Toronto, Ontario M4P 2Y3.*

In Australia: Please write to *Penguin Books Australia Ltd, P.O. Box 257, Ringwood, Victoria 3134.*

In New Zealand: Please write to *Penguin Books (NZ) Ltd, Private Bag 102902, North Shore Mail Centre, Auckland 10.*

In India: Please write to *Penguin Books India Pvt Ltd, 11 Panchsheel Shopping Centre, Panchsheel Park, New Delhi 110 017.*

In the Netherlands: Please write to *Penguin Books Netherlands bv, Postbus 3507, NL-1001 AH Amsterdam.*

In Germany: Please write to *Penguin Books Deutschland GmbH, Metzlerstrasse 26, 60594 Frankfurt am Main.*

In Spain: Please write to *Penguin Books S. A., Bravo Murillo 19, 1° B, 28015 Madrid.*

In Italy: Please write to *Penguin Italia s.r.l., Via Benedetto Croce 2, 20094 Corsico, Milano.*

In France: Please write to *Penguin France, Le Carré Wilson, 62 rue Benjamin Baillaud, 31500 Toulouse.*

In Japan: Please write to *Penguin Books Japan Ltd, Kaneko Building, 2-3-25 Koraku, Bunkyo-Ku, Tokyo 112.*

In South Africa: Please write to *Penguin Books South Africa (Pty) Ltd, Private Bag X14, Parkview, 2122 Johannesburg.*